CHRIST ABOVE ALL

A Study in Colossians

ROBERT GRIFFITH

GRACE AND TRUTH PUBLISHING
PO Box 338, Gunnedah NSW 2380 Australia
www.graceandtruthpublishing.com.au

All Bible quotes are from the
New International Version (NIV)
expect where otherwise stated.

Quotes in square brackets are the author's comment.

ISBN 978-1-7646132-0-0

TABLE OF CONTENTS

1. THE GOSPEL THAT BEARS FRUIT EVERYWHERE
(Colossians 1:1-14)

Paul opens his letter to the Colossians not with abstraction or argument, but with gratitude. Before he addresses any error, confusion, or moral challenge, he gives thanks to God for what is already evident among them. This is not flattery, nor is this a rhetorical softening before his rebuke.

It is a clear theological declaration. Paul wants the Colossians to understand that the Christian life does not begin with what we do for God, but with what God has already done in Christ, and how that work is already bearing fruit among them. From the very first lines, the gospel is framed not as a fragile thing that must be protected by human effort, but as a living, powerful reality that produces visible transformation wherever it takes root.

Paul first identifies himself as "an apostle of Christ Jesus by the will of God." (Colossians 1:1). His authority does not rest on personal ambition, ecclesiastical appointment, or spiritual charisma. It rests on the will of God. That matters because everything that follows in this letter flows from that conviction: Christ is supreme, Christ is sufficient, and the Church belongs to Him.

Timothy is mentioned alongside Paul, not as a co-author in the technical sense, but as a trusted co-worker whose life and ministry confirm the same gospel. Even in the greeting, there is already a sense of shared faith, shared mission, and shared dependence on Christ.

The recipients are described as "God's holy people in Colossae, the faithful brothers and sisters in Christ." (Colossians 1:2). Paul does not begin by addressing their problems. He addresses their identity. They are holy, not because they have achieved moral perfection, but because they belong to God. They are faithful, not because they never struggle, but because they remain in Christ. This is crucial for understanding the rest of this letter.

Colossians will confront false teaching, spiritual pressure, and distorted views of maturity, but it will do so by anchoring believers in who they already are in Christ, not by placing them on a treadmill of religious striving.

Paul's greeting culminates in a familiar but deeply significant blessing: "Grace and peace to you from God our Father." (Colossians 1:2). Grace comes first, because true peace is never achieved apart from grace. Peace with God can only flow from God's grace – God's empowering presence, never from human performance. Even at the outset, the great Apostle is shaping the theological instincts of his readers. The Christian life is not sustained by adding new religious techniques, but by living more deeply in the grace already given.

Thanksgiving rooted in the work of God

Paul's thanksgiving is directed explicitly to God. "We always thank God, the Father of our Lord Jesus Christ, when we pray for you." (Colossians 1:3). The fruit evident in the Colossian Church does not cause Paul to congratulate them; it causes him to worship God.

That distinction is subtle but essential. When genuine spiritual growth occurs, the proper response is not self-congratulation but praise to God. Paul recognises that faith, love, and hope are not self-generated virtues. They are gifts produced by the gospel at work within a community.

The content of Paul's thanksgiving is specific. He gives thanks because he has heard of their faith in Christ Jesus and of the love they have for all God's people (Colossians 1:4). Faith and love are always inseparable in Paul's theology.

Faith in Christ always expresses itself in love for others. A faith that remains abstract, private, or disconnected from tangible love is not the faith Paul is describing. The Colossians' faith has direction - it is "in Christ Jesus." Their love has breadth - it is "for all God's people." This already stands in quiet contrast to the exclusivity and elitism that often accompany false spirituality.

Paul then introduces hope as the foundation beneath both faith and love. "The faith and love that spring from the hope stored up for you in heaven." (Colossians 1:5). Hope is not presented as wishful thinking about the future. It is a settled confidence grounded in what God has promised and secured. Paul says hope is "stored up" for them, indicating security, permanence, and divine preservation. It is not fragile, nor is it dependent on their continued performance. Because their future is secure in Christ, their present lives are marked by faith and love.

This hope is not a new revelation or some kind of secret teaching. Paul is careful to say that they have already heard of this hope "in the true message of the gospel that has come to you." (Colossians 1:5). From the outset, Paul draws a clear line between the gospel they received and any later claims to deeper or higher spiritual knowledge. The gospel is true, sufficient, and complete. There is no second-tier version reserved for the spiritually advanced.

The Gospel that bears fruit everywhere

Paul now broadens the horizon beyond Colossae. "In the same way, the gospel is bearing fruit and growing throughout the whole world, just as it has been doing among you since the day you heard it and truly understood God's grace." (Colossians 1:6).

This is one of the most expansive statements in the letter. The gospel is not confined to one culture, one ethnicity, or one spiritual style. It is alive and active across the world, producing the same kind of fruit wherever it is received in truth.

Two important features of the gospel stand out here: it bears fruit, and it also grows. Fruit speaks of visible transformation - changed lives, renewed relationships and practical obedience. Growth speaks of expansion and endurance. The gospel does not stagnate. It moves outward, and it goes deeper. Paul deliberately connects the Colossians' experience with the global work of God. They are not an isolated experiment; they are part of something vast and ongoing.

Importantly, Paul ties this fruitfulness to understanding grace. The gospel has been bearing fruit among them "since the day you heard it and truly understood God's grace." (Colossians 1:6).

Growth in the Christian life is not driven by fear, guilt, or pressure, but by a deepening grasp of God's amazing grace. When grace is misunderstood, distorted, or replaced with rule-keeping, spiritual vitality withers. Where grace is known and embraced, fruit always follows.

Paul's emphasis here would have been especially important in Colossae, where believers were being tempted to supplement the gospel with additional spiritual practices. Paul insists that the same gospel that saved them is the gospel that sustains them. There is no other engine for growth.

A faithful servant and a shared ministry

Paul names Epaphras as the one through whom the Colossians first learned the gospel. "You learned it from Epaphras, our dear fellow servant, who is a faithful minister of Christ on our behalf." (Colossians 1:7). This brief reference carries significant weight. Paul is affirming Epaphras publicly, calling him faithful and identifying his ministry as genuinely Christ-centred. In doing so, Paul reinforces continuity.

The message the Colossians received from Epaphras is the same message Paul proclaims. Epaphras is not presented as a spiritual innovator or a charismatic personality. He is a servant, a minister, and a messenger of Jesus Christ. His faithfulness lies in delivering the gospel, not embellishing it. Paul's affirmation would have reassured the Colossians that they had not missed out on something essential, nor had they been given an inferior version of the truth.

Paul concludes this section by noting that Epaphras has informed him of their love in the Spirit (Colossians 1:8). This is not merely human affection or social cohesion. It is the love produced by the Holy Spirit, rooted in the gospel, and directed toward others.

Even before Paul begins to address doctrinal concerns or ethical instructions, he establishes this foundation: God is already at work among them, the gospel is already bearing fruit, and their lives already testify to its power.

From the very beginning, this letter to the Colossians calls believers away from insecurity and toward confidence in Christ. The gospel they have received is not lacking. It is alive, it is powerful, and it is sufficient. For this reason, Paul's thanksgiving naturally gives way to intercession. Gratitude for what God has already done does not lead to passivity; it deepens prayer.

Hearing of their faith and love has not convinced him that nothing more is needed. Instead, it has clarified what kind of growth truly matters. The concern now is not whether the Colossians will acquire new spiritual experiences, but whether they will grow in a deeper grasp of God's will and live lives shaped by it.

The prayer is introduced with deliberate persistence. "For this reason, since the day we heard about you, we have not stopped praying for you." (Colossians 1:9). The language here signals sustained concern rather than a passing thought. Paul is not offering a polite blessing; he is describing an ongoing pastoral burden. What follows reveals his priorities, and they are strikingly different from the spiritual aspirations often promoted in religious settings.

The central request is clear: "We continually ask God to fill you with the knowledge of His will through all the wisdom and understanding that the Spirit gives." (Colossians 1:9). Knowledge here is not abstract information. It is relational and practical, rooted in God's revealed purposes.

This prayer does not ask for secret insight, mystical visions, or elite understanding available only to a few. The knowledge of God's will comes through wisdom and understanding given by the Spirit, not through human innovation. This is especially important in the context of Colossae.

The pressure facing these believers was not atheism or outright denial of Christ, but the suggestion that something more was needed. Paul counters that heresy directly. God's will is not hidden behind layers of religious technique. It is made known by the Spirit to ordinary believers who belong to Christ.

A life that pleases the Lord

The purpose of this prayer is immediately stated. "So that you may live a life worthy of the Lord and please Him in every way." (Colossians 1:10). Knowledge is never an end in itself. True understanding always leads somewhere. A life worthy of the Lord is not about earning approval, but about living in a manner that reflects the reality of belonging to Christ. Pleasing God flows from relationship, not performance.

Paul then describes what such a life looks like. First, it is a life that is fruitful. Believers are called to be "bearing fruit in every good work." (Colossians 1:10). This echoes the earlier description of the gospel itself bearing fruit. What the gospel does globally, it also does personally. Good works are not the root of salvation, but they are its inevitable fruit.

Second, this life involves growth. There is an ongoing process of "growing in the knowledge of God." (Colossians 1:10). Growth is not portrayed as moving beyond the gospel, but as going deeper into knowing God himself. Christian maturity is always relational before it is behavioural. The goal is not mastery of religious concepts, but a deeper acquaintance with the God who has made himself known in Christ.

Strength for endurance, not escape

The prayer then turns toward endurance. "Being strengthened with all power according to His glorious might so that you may have great endurance and patience." (Colossians 1:11). Strength is requested, but not for dominance, influence, or personal success. It is strength for perseverance. Endurance and patience are needed precisely because the Christian life involves pressure, opposition, and suffering.

Paul does not assume that spiritual growth removes all the difficulties. Instead, he assumes the opposite. Faithfulness will require sustained strength that only God can supply to us. The source of that strength is God's glorious might, never human resolve. Endurance is not stoicism; it is dependence.

This endurance is marked by joy. The phrase that follows is easy to miss, but deeply significant: "and giving joyful thanks to the Father." (Colossians 1:12). Joy and gratitude are not postponed until circumstances improve. They are woven into endurance itself. The Christian life is not about grim survival until relief comes, but about confident trust in the midst of difficulty.

Qualified by grace, not achievement

Gratitude is directed specifically to the Father, "who has qualified you to share in the inheritance of His holy people in the kingdom of light." (Colossians 1:12). The language is decisive. Qualification is something God has already done. It is not something believers achieve through effort or maturity. The inheritance is shared, not earned, and it belongs to those who are part of God's people.

This statement directly undermines any teaching that divides Christians into spiritual classes. There is no suggestion that only some are qualified, or that qualification increases with advanced practice. Every believer in Christ shares fully in the inheritance. The kingdom of light is not reserved for the spiritually elite.

The contrast with what follows sharpens the point. "For He has rescued us from the dominion of darkness and brought us into the kingdom of the Son He loves." (Colossians 1:13). Our salvation is described as deliverance and transfer. Darkness is not merely ignorance; it is dominion. Humanity does not drift neutrally until it finds the light. It must be rescued.

The movement is decisive and complete. Believers have been brought into another kingdom altogether. This new realm is defined not merely by light, but by relationship. It is the kingdom of the Son whom the Father loves. Security rests not only in power, but in love.

Redemption accomplished in Christ

The prayer reaches its theological centre with a simple but profound declaration. "In whom we have redemption, the forgiveness of sins." (Colossians 1:14). Redemption is not future possibility; it is present reality. Forgiveness is not partial or provisional; it is complete. Everything that follows in the letter about Christ's supremacy and sufficiency flows from this truth.

Paul does not treat forgiveness as a preliminary step that must later be supplemented. It stands at the heart of the Christian life. Sin has been dealt with. Guilt has been removed. Relationship with God has been restored. There is nothing lacking that needs to be filled by additional spiritual systems.

This prayer, taken as a whole, reshapes the Colossians' understanding of maturity. Growth is not about moving beyond Christ, but about living more fully in Christ. Knowledge leads to obedience. Strength produces endurance. Gratitude flows from grace. The Christian life is not sustained by fear of inadequacy, but by confidence in what God has already accomplished. By praying this way, Paul gently but firmly redirects their attention. The issue is not whether Christ is enough. The real question is whether they will continue to live in light of what they have already received by God's grace.

The movement of thought in this opening section reaches its deepest point not in instruction, but in assurance. Everything said so far presses toward confidence rather than anxiety. Faith, love, hope, endurance, and gratitude all flow from one decisive reality: God has already acted. The Christian life begins not with what believers must do, but with what God has done for them in Christ. Paul wants the Colossians to live from that centre, not drift away from it.

The language of rescue is especially telling. "For He has rescued us from the dominion of darkness." (Colossians 1:13). Darkness is not described as a neutral condition or some temporary phase. It is a dominion - a realm of authority and control. Humanity is not portrayed as spiritually lost but otherwise free.

It is portrayed as captive. This is why salvation must always be described as rescue rather than self-discovery. No amount of insight, discipline, or religious effort can free someone from a dominion. Deliverance must come from outside.

That rescue, however, is not merely an escape. It is also a transfer. God has "brought us into the kingdom of the Son He loves." (Colossians 1:13). Salvation is not simply being saved from something, but being brought into something. A new kingdom, a new allegiance, and a new identity now define the believer's life. This kingdom is not described primarily in terms of rules or rituals, but in terms of relationship. It belongs to the Son, and that Son is loved by the Father. To belong to this kingdom is to be caught up in that love.

This shift in kingdoms is decisive. Paul does not speak of a gradual transition or a probationary period. Believers have been brought in. The action is now complete. This matters deeply for a Church facing pressure to improve its spiritual standing. You cannot be half-rescued or partially transferred. Either you remain under the dominion of darkness, or you belong to the kingdom of the Son. There is no intermediate spiritual status.

At the heart of this rescue stands redemption. "In whom we have redemption, the forgiveness of sins." (Colossians 1:14). The term redemption is very rich, drawing from the language of release, payment, and freedom. It assumes bondage and speaks of cost. Forgiveness is not achieved by ignoring sin or by minimising its seriousness. It is accomplished through decisive action on God's part. Though Paul will later unfold the cosmic significance of Christ's work, he begins here with what every believer knows personally: sin is forgiven.

The tense here is important. Redemption is something believers <u>have</u>, not something they are waiting to receive. Forgiveness is not provisional, nor is it dependent on reaching a higher level of maturity. This statement quietly but powerfully undermines any teaching that treats forgiveness as an entry-level benefit that must later be supplemented by deeper spiritual achievements.

There is nothing superficial about forgiveness. It lies at the centre of the gospel. Throughout this opening section of the letter, Paul has been shaping how the Colossians think about growth. Growth does not mean leaving the gospel behind. It means living more fully within it.

The prayer for knowledge, wisdom, and understanding does not move them beyond Christ, but deeper into the implications of belonging to Christ. Every element of the Christian life described here flows from grace, not from anxiety or expectation.

That perspective remains deeply relevant. Whenever believers feel the pressure to measure themselves against others, to compare spiritual experiences, or to chase a longed-for sense of completeness elsewhere, the same temptation is at work.

The danger is subtle. It rarely comes as a rejection of Christ, but as an addition to Him. Paul's opening words are designed to guard against that drift before it takes hold. Notice how often God is the active subject in these verses.

God fills with knowledge. God strengthens with power. God qualifies for inheritance. God rescues from darkness. God brings us into the kingdom. Redemption is found in Christ, not manufactured by effort. This repeated emphasis is not accidental. It is pastoral. It lifts the weight of self-salvation from the shoulders of the Church and places it where it belongs.

At the same time, this assurance does not lead to passivity. The prayer assumes obedience, endurance, and fruitfulness. A life worthy of the Lord is still the goal. But that life grows out of confidence, not insecurity. Obedience becomes a response to grace rather than a strategy for earning acceptance. Endurance becomes possible because strength comes from God's glorious might, not from human resolve.

The connection between gratitude and perseverance is especially important. Giving thanks is not something reserved for moments of success or comfort. It is woven into the life of faith precisely because the decisive work has already been done.

Gratitude flows from knowing where one stands. Those who are uncertain of their place before God will always struggle to give thanks freely. Those who know they are rescued, forgiven, and brought into the kingdom of God, can give thanks even when circumstances are hard.

By the time this opening section closes, the foundation has been laid. Before false teaching is exposed, before ethical instruction is given, and before the supremacy of Christ is unfolded in its full glory, the Church is reminded of what is already true. They are in Christ. They are forgiven. They belong to a new kingdom. The gospel they received is alive, powerful, and sufficient.

Paul has not yet named the specific challenges facing the Colossians, but he has already prepared them to face those challenges with confidence. The question is no longer whether Christ is enough. The real issue is whether they will continue to live as people who believe that He is. Everything that follows in the letter will press that question more deeply, but it will never move beyond this foundation.

How then shall we live?

Paul's opening thanksgiving and prayer in Colossians 1:1–14 is not a theological warm-up before the 'real' teaching begins. It establishes the shape of Christian discipleship from the very outset.

Before Paul addresses error, ethics, or endurance, he grounds the Christian life in grace received, faith exercised, hope secured, and fruit borne. If we are to live faithfully as disciples of Christ today, we must allow this opening vision to recalibrate both our expectations and our priorities.

First, we are reminded that the Christian life begins not with effort but with **grace**. Paul addresses the Colossians as "holy and faithful brothers and sisters in Christ." (Colossians 1:2). That description is not aspirational; it is declarative. They are holy because they belong to Christ, not because they have achieved moral perfection.

For modern disciples, this is foundational. We do not live the Christian life in order to become accepted by God; we live it because we already are accepted in Christ. This frees us from anxious striving and also from forms of performance-driven spirituality. Discipleship flows from identity, not insecurity.

Second, Paul shows us that genuine faith always expresses itself **relationally**. He gives thanks because he has heard of the Colossians' faith in Christ Jesus and their love for all God's people (Colossians 1:4). Faith that remains purely private or inward is not the faith Paul celebrates. To live as disciples today means recognising that love for Christ and love for His people cannot be separated.

Church involvement is not an optional extra for mature Christians; it is a natural expression of gospel faith. Discipleship is personal, but it is never solitary.

Third, Paul anchors present obedience in **future hope**. Faith and love, he says, "spring from the hope stored up for you in heaven." (Colossians 1:5). The Christian life is sustained by a future that is secure and promised. In a world dominated by immediacy, fear, and uncertainty, disciples of Christ live differently because they know where history is heading. Our hope is not wishful thinking, nor is it escapism. It is a settled confidence that shapes how we endure suffering, resist temptation, and persevere in obedience. We live patiently now because our future is certain.

Fourth, Paul insists that the gospel is not static but **fruit-bearing**. "All over the world this gospel is bearing fruit and growing." (Colossians 1:6). The same gospel that saves also transforms. To live as disciples today is to expect change – not instant perfection, but real growth.

A Christianity that leaves us unchanged in character, priorities, or desires is not the gospel Paul proclaims. Growth in Christ is gradual, often uneven, but unmistakably real. Discipleship means submitting ourselves to the ongoing work of God's grace in us.

Fifth, Paul's prayer gives us a clear vision of **spiritual maturity**. He does not pray for comfort, success, or ease, but that believers may be filled with the knowledge of God's will, live lives worthy of the Lord, bear fruit in every good work, grow in the knowledge of God, and be strengthened with all power to endure (Colossians 1:9–11). This challenges many modern assumptions. Discipleship is not primarily about self-fulfilment or religious experience. It is about a life increasingly shaped by God's will, marked by perseverance, and characterised by grateful obedience.

Sixth, Paul reminds us that endurance is sustained by **gratitude**. He speaks of believers "giving joyful thanks to the Father." (Colossians 1:12). Gratitude is not emotional optimism; it is theological realism. We give thanks because God has already acted decisively on our behalf. He has qualified us to share in the inheritance of His people, rescued us from the dominion of darkness, and brought us into the kingdom of His Son (Colossians 1:12–13). Discipleship today is sustained not by constant innovation, but by continual remembrance of what God has already done.

Finally, Paul locates all Christian living within the reality of **redemption in Christ**. "In whom we have redemption, the forgiveness of sins." (Colossians 1:14). Everything flows from this. We live forgiven lives, not condemned ones. We pursue holiness not to earn redemption, but because redemption has already been granted. We resist sin not out of fear, but out of freedom.

So how then shall we live? We live as people who know who we are in Christ. We live as members of a loving community shaped by gospel hope. We live expectantly, bearing fruit as the gospel takes deeper root in our lives. We live patiently, strengthened by God's power for endurance. We live gratefully, remembering that we have already been rescued and redeemed. This is not an abstract ideal. It is the ordinary, faithful shape of discipleship for those who belong to Christ today.

The opening prayer has firmly established confidence in the gospel and assurance in what God has already done. Now the focus tightens, not by narrowing the vision, but by lifting it higher. Attention is drawn decisively to the person of Christ himself. If the Colossians are being tempted to supplement their faith with additional practices, intermediaries, or spiritual systems, the most effective response is not argument but revelation. Paul does not begin by dismantling false ideas one by one. He sets Christ before them in all His glory and all His sufficiency, thereby allowing everything else to be measured against Him.

What follows now is one of the most profound Christological passages in the New Testament. It's not a detached theological essay, but a carefully shaped declaration designed to stabilise a Church under pressure. The issue at stake is not simply correct doctrine, but the very centre of the Christian life. If Christ is misunderstood, diminished, or placed alongside other powers, everything else will eventually distort. If Christ is seen rightly, the rest of the letter will fall into place.

The description begins with a statement in Colossians 1:15, that reaches back to the deepest questions of human existence. "The Son is the image of the invisible God, the firstborn over all creation." God is invisible, God is beyond human sight and comprehension. Yet in Christ, God has made Himself known. This is not just a partial reflection or a vague representation. To see the Son is to see what God is like. Jesus does not merely speak about God; He reveals Him.

The image of the invisible God

The word 'image' is rich with meaning. It doesn't suggest resemblance alone, but visible manifestation. In Christ, the character, authority, and nature of God are made accessible. This directly challenges any spirituality that looks elsewhere for fuller revelation.

There is no deeper picture of God hidden behind Christ, no higher truth beyond Him. Everything God intends to show of Himself is revealed in the Son.

The phrase "firstborn over all creation" has sometimes been misunderstood, as though it implies that Christ is part of creation. That is precisely the opposite of the point being made. In biblical language, "firstborn" speaks of status and authority, not origin. It denotes supremacy, inheritance, and rule. Christ stands *over* creation, His is not *within* creation. He holds the rights of the firstborn, exercising lordship over all that exists. This authority is immediately explained in the next verse.

"For in Him all things were created: things in heaven and on earth, visible and invisible, whether thrones or powers or rulers or authorities." (Colossians 1:16). Nothing is excluded. The visible world, the unseen spiritual realm, and every structure of power fall within the scope of His creative work. The very categories that might have fascinated or intimidated the Colossians are named and subordinated to Christ.

Creation is not only through Him, but also for Him. "All things have been created through Him and for Him." (Colossians 1:16). Purpose as well as origin is addressed here. Everything exists with reference to Christ. Nothing has an independent centre. This means that no spiritual power, no human authority, and no religious system can claim ultimate significance. All find their meaning in relation to Him.

Christ before all things

The declaration continues by pressing the point even further. "He is before all things, and in him all things hold together." (Colossians 1:17). Christ does not merely initiate creation and then step back. He sustains it. The coherence of the universe depends on him. Every moment of continued existence is an act of his sustaining power. This has profound implications for faith. The one in whom believers trust is not limited to the private or spiritual realm. He is actively involved in the ongoing order of all things.

The same Christ who forgives sins also holds the universe together. There is no competition between cosmic authority and personal care. They belong to the same person.

At this point, the focus shifts from creation to the Church. "And He is the head of the body, the Church." (Colossians 1:18). The transition is deliberate. The one who reigns over all creation also governs His redeemed people. The Church is not a voluntary association or a human organisation seeking direction. It is a body with a living head. Direction, life, and unity flow from Christ Himself.

This headship is not symbolic or distant. It implies active leadership and intimate connection. The life of the Church depends entirely on its ongoing relationship with Christ. Any attempt to define maturity, authority, or spirituality apart from Him, severs the body from its source of life.

The description then returns to the language of firstness. "He is the beginning and the firstborn from among the dead." (Colossians 1:18). Resurrection stands at the centre here. Christ's supremacy is not only demonstrated in creation, but also in new creation. He is the first to rise in a way that guarantees resurrection for others. His victory over death establishes Him as supreme in a realm where human power always fails.

The purpose of all this is now stated very plainly: "So that in everything He might have the supremacy." (Colossians 1:18). This is the controlling aim. Not partial authority. Not shared dominance. Supremacy in everything. Any teaching, practice, or devotion that diminishes that supremacy is exposed as inadequate, no matter how impressive it may appear.

The fullness of God in Christ

The next statement grounds Christ's supremacy in the will of God himself. "For God was pleased to have all His fullness dwell in Him." (Colossians 1:19). Fullness is not divided, distributed, or shared across spiritual realms. It dwells entirely in Christ. Everything that makes God who He is finds its dwelling place in the Son.

This directly challenges any ideas that will treat Christ as one mediator among many, or as a starting point toward greater spiritual realities. There is no remainder of divine fullness elsewhere. God has not held anything back. The pleasure of God rests in this complete self-giving.

That fullness is not static. It is expressed in reconciliation. "And through Him to reconcile to Himself all things, whether things on earth or things in heaven, by making peace through His blood, shed on the cross." (Colossians 1:20).

The scope of reconciliation matches the scope of creation. Sin has disrupted everything, and God's response is not limited to isolated individuals. The cross has cosmic significance. Peace is not achieved through negotiation or gradual improvement. It is made through bloodshed.

The cross stands at the centre of reconciliation, confronting the seriousness of sin and the depth of God's love. Any spirituality that avoids the cross, downplays it, or moves beyond it, has lost its anchor.

Here, the theological vision narrows once again to address the personal experience of the Colossians themselves. What is true of the cosmos is also true of them. The Christ who reconciles all things has reconciled them.

This movement from cosmic to personal sets the stage for what follows. The supremacy of Christ is not an abstract doctrine. It reshapes how believers understand their past, their present, and their future. Before ethical instruction is given, before warnings are issued, and before practical application unfolds, the foundation is laid where it must always be laid: in a clear, uncompromising vision of who Christ is.

Everything else in the letter will rest on this. If Christ truly is the image of the invisible God, the creator and sustainer of all things, the head of the Church, the firstborn from the dead, and the one in whom all fullness dwells, then there is nothing He cannot address and nothing He cannot supply.

However, the vision of Christ's supremacy does not remain suspended in the heavens. Having declared who Christ is in relation to God, creation, and the Church, the focus now turns toward the lived reality of those who belong to Him. The movement is deliberate. Cosmic truth is never detached from personal transformation. What Christ has accomplished on a universal scale has direct and decisive implications for ordinary believers in Colossae.

The shift is marked by a stark reminder of their former condition. "Once you were alienated from God and were enemies in your minds because of your evil behaviour." (Colossians 1:21). The language is strong and intentionally unsettling. Alienation describes separation, distance, and exclusion. Enmity goes further. It describes hostility, not neutrality. Humanity is not portrayed as merely ignorant of God, but opposed to Him. That opposition is rooted not only in actions, but in the mind itself. Sin distorts understanding as well as behaviour.

This description prevents any sentimental view of salvation. Reconciliation is not a polite reconciliation between equals who have drifted apart. It is the restoration of those who were actively opposed to God. By naming this reality plainly, Paul ensures that grace is not trivialised. The depth of the problem magnifies the magnitude of God's response.

Reconciled through a real body

Against this dark backdrop, the gospel shines with particular clarity. "But now He has reconciled you by Christ's physical body through death." (Colossians 1:22).

The contrast here could not be sharper. Alienation gives way to reconciliation. Enmity is replaced with peace. The means of that reconciliation is explicitly stated. It is accomplished through Christ's physical body and through death.

This emphasis matters. In a context where some were tempted to spiritualise Christ or diminish the significance of his true humanity, the reality of His physical body is non-negotiable.

Salvation is not achieved through abstract spiritual principles, but through a real death in a real body. The cross is not symbolic. It is historical, concrete, and central.

The purpose of this reconciliation is also clearly defined. It is "to present you holy in His sight, without blemish and free from accusation." (Colossians 1:22). This is courtroom language. The believer stands before God not as a defendant hoping for leniency, but as one declared clean.

Holiness here is not a future aspiration, it is a present standing. Freedom from accusation does not depend on our flawless performance, but on Christ's finished work.

This is a decisive statement of assurance. Any system that keeps believers perpetually uncertain of their standing before God stands in tension with this declaration. The gospel does not leave room for lingering accusations. Christ's reconciliation is sufficient to silence them.

Holding fast to the Gospel

At this point, a necessary exhortation is introduced. "If you continue in your faith, established and firm, and do not move from the hope held out in the gospel." (Colossians 1:23). This is not a threat designed to provoke fear, but a call to perseverance. The issue is not earning salvation, but remaining grounded in the truth that has already saved them.

Continuing in faith does not mean progressing beyond the gospel. It means refusing to drift away from it. The imagery is architectural. Faith is to be established and firm, not shifting or unstable. The danger facing the Colossians is not moral collapse, but theological displacement. The hope held out in the gospel is sufficient, but it can be abandoned if believers are persuaded that something else is needed.

Paul reinforces this point by again widening the horizon. This gospel "has been proclaimed to every creature under heaven." (Colossians 1:23).

The message they received is not a localised or experimental version. It belongs to the universal mission of God. Their faith is anchored not only in personal experience, but in the worldwide proclamation of Christ.

The personal note that follows is subtle but important. Paul describes himself as a servant of this gospel. His authority does not elevate him above it. He is bound to the same message he proclaims. This reinforces a consistent theme: no teacher, no leader, and no experience stands above the gospel itself.

Suffering that serves the Church

What follows may seem surprising. Having just celebrated reconciliation and assurance, the letter turns to suffering. "Now I rejoice in what I am suffering for you." (Colossians 1:24). Rejoicing in suffering is not natural. It requires a framework that gives suffering meaning. Paul does not glorify pain for its own sake. He rejoices because his suffering serves the Church.

The phrase that follows has generated much discussion. Paul speaks of "filling up in my flesh what is still lacking in regard to Christ's afflictions." (Colossians 1:24). This does not imply that Christ's saving work is incomplete. Nothing is lacking in the atonement. The context makes that clear. What is lacking is not redemptive value, but ongoing representation. Christ's sufferings continue in the sense that His body, the Church, continues to face opposition in the world.

Paul's sufferings are not an addition to Christ's work, but a participation in it. As the gospel advances, it will encounter resistance. Those who carry it share in that cost. This suffering is described as being "for the sake of His body, which is the Church." (Colossians 1:24). The focus is corporate. Even here, individual experience is framed in terms of service to others.

This understanding of suffering would have challenged any teaching equating spiritual maturity with comfort, protection, or exemption from hardship. Faithfulness does not guarantee ease. It often invites opposition. But suffering endured for the sake of the gospel is never meaningless.

A stewardship entrusted by God

In Colossians 1:25, Paul now describes his role in terms of stewardship. He has become a servant of the Church "by the commission God gave me to present to you the word of God in its fullness." The phrase "word of God in its fullness" is especially significant. It stands in direct contrast to claims of hidden knowledge or supplementary revelation.

The gospel entrusted to Paul is complete. Nothing essential is withheld. This fullness does not mean that every mystery is immediately understood. The next verse speaks of "the mystery that has been kept hidden for ages and generations but is now disclosed to the Lord's people." (Colossians 1:26).

Mystery in biblical terms does not refer to something that is permanently obscure. It refers to something once hidden and now revealed by God's initiative. That mystery is then named. "Christ in you, the hope of glory." (Colossians 1:27). This is the heart of the gospel. God's saving presence is not distant or occasional. It dwells within His people. Hope is not grounded in human potential, but in Christ's indwelling presence. Glory is not something believers strive to reach alone. It is something promised because Christ is already at work within them.

This truth would have directly countered any teaching that encouraged believers to seek spiritual fullness elsewhere. Fullness is not found by ascending spiritual ladders, but by recognising who already dwells within. Christ in you is not the starting point to be left behind. It is the centre to be embraced.

The scope of this revelation is emphasised. It is made known "among the Gentiles" (Colossians 1:27). What was once confined to Israel's hopes has now expanded to include all nations. The gospel is not ethnically or culturally restricted. The same Christ dwells in all who believe. Here, Paul prepares the way for the pastoral aim that will follow. If Christ truly is supreme over all creation, sufficient for reconciliation, present within His people, and proclaimed fully in the gospel, then there is no need to look elsewhere for completeness.

The foundation is being laid carefully and deliberately. The call that remains is to live in light of what is already true. The revelation of the mystery does not remain theoretical. Having declared that Christ dwells within his people as the hope of glory, the focus now turns to purpose and labour. Truth revealed by God always presses toward transformation. The presence of Christ within believers reshapes how ministry is understood, how growth is pursued, and how perseverance is sustained.

Paul describes the centre of his own ministry with deliberate clarity. "He is the one we proclaim, admonishing and teaching everyone with all wisdom." (Colossians 1:28). The object of proclamation is not a system of ethics, a philosophical framework, or a set of spiritual techniques. It is a person. Jesus Christ stands at the centre of everything proclaimed. Teaching and warning are not ends in themselves. They serve the greater aim of making Christ known and understood.

The scope of this ministry is equally striking. It is directed toward "everyone." There is no restricted audience, no inner circle of advanced believers. The wisdom involved is not secret knowledge reserved for the few, but wisdom applied universally. This stands in sharp contrast to any spirituality that thrives on exclusivity. In Christ, maturity is not gated by status, background, or experience.

Maturity defined by Christlikeness

The goal of this proclamation is explicitly stated: "so that we may present everyone fully mature in Christ." (Colossians 1:28). Maturity is not measured by spiritual experiences, religious achievements, or ascetic discipline. It is measured by union with Christ. To be mature is to belong to Him fully, to be shaped increasingly by His life and character.

The phrase "in Christ" is quite decisive. Maturity does not mean moving beyond Christ, but being more deeply rooted in Him. This corrects a subtle but dangerous misconception. Growth is not a linear ascent away from the gospel, but a deepening engagement with the gospel.

Any definition of maturity that shifts the focus away from Christ inevitably distorts the Christian life. This vision of maturity also guards against despair. If maturity depended on extraordinary achievement, many would feel excluded. But if maturity is defined by relationship with Christ, it becomes accessible to all believers. Growth may look different in different lives, but the centre remains the same.

Labour empowered by Christ's strength

Paul then speaks candidly about the cost of this ministry. "To this end I strenuously contend with all the energy Christ so powerfully works in me." (Colossians 1:29). So, ministry is described as labour and struggle. There is effort involved. The Christian life is not effortless drift. Yet the source of energy is crucial. The labour is real, but the strength is not self-generated.

This balance is essential. On the one hand, passivity is rejected. Paul contends, strives, and works. On the other hand, self-reliance is equally rejected. The energy at work within him belongs to Christ. What Christ requires, Christ supplies. The effort required of believers is always matched by the power provided by God.

This understanding protects against two common errors. One is burnout driven by self-reliance, where responsibility is carried without dependence on Christ. The other is complacency disguised as trust, where effort is avoided under the guise of faith. Paul's model holds effort and dependence together. The emphasis on Christ's power also reinforces the letter's central theme. Supremacy does not end with authority over creation. It extends into the ongoing life of the Church. The same Christ who sustains the universe sustains each of His servants. There is no division between cosmic power and personal enablement.

A vision that anchors the Church

As this section draws to a close, the threads of the argument begin to converge. Christ is supreme over creation. Christ is sufficient for reconciliation. Christ dwells within His people.

Christ is the centre of proclamation. Christ defines maturity. Christ supplies strength. Nothing essential lies outside of Him. This comprehensive vision addresses the Colossians' situation with pastoral wisdom. Rather than attacking false teaching head-on, Paul establishes a framework in which such teaching loses its appeal. When Christ is seen clearly, alternatives lose their attraction. When His fullness is truly understood, additions become unnecessary.

The implications for the Church are far-reaching. Identity is anchored in Christ, not in practices or philosophies. Growth is measured by closeness to Him, not by the many external markers. Endurance is sustained by His power, not by human resilience. Confidence rests in His completed work, not in ongoing spiritual performance.

This vision also reshapes how believers view their own struggles. Effort is not a sign of failure, and weakness is not a contradiction of faith. Striving in dependence on Christ is normal Christian living. The goal is not self-sufficiency, but faithfulness.

As Paul's letter continues, practical exhortations and warnings will follow. The pressure to adopt alternative spiritual frameworks will be addressed directly. But none of that will make sense apart from this foundation. The supremacy of Christ is not an abstract doctrine to be admired. It is the living centre from which the Christian life flows. Paul's labour, prayer, and proclamation all serve one purpose: that believers would stand complete in Christ. That same aim remains vital. Wherever the Church is tempted to look elsewhere for fullness, the answer is not novelty, but clarity. Christ is enough. He always has been.

How then shall we live?

Colossians 1:15–23 confronts us with one of the most expansive and demanding visions of Jesus Christ in all of Scripture. Paul does not present Christ as merely helpful, inspiring, or spiritually significant. He presents Him as supreme – over creation, over redemption, over the Church, and over history itself.

If this is who Christ truly is, then discipleship today cannot remain casual, compartmentalised, or selective. This passage forces each and every one of us to ask what it actually means to live under the lordship of such a Christ.

First, we are called to live with a **Christ-shaped view of reality**. Paul declares that Christ is the image of the invisible God, the firstborn over all creation, and the one through whom and for whom all things were made (Colossians 1:15–16). For modern disciples, this challenges the habit of treating Jesus as relevant only to "spiritual" matters.

If all things were created through Him and for Him, then no area of our life is neutral territory. Work, relationships, decisions, ambitions, suffering, and even the created world itself must be understood in relation to Christ. To live as disciples today is to resist a fragmented life and to learn to see everything through the lens of Christ's supremacy.

Second, this passage calls us to live with **deep confidence rather than quiet anxiety**. Paul insists that "in Him all things hold together" (Colossians 1:17). That is not poetic exaggeration. It is a theological claim about reality. In a world that often feels unstable, fractured, and unpredictable, disciples of Christ are invited to live without panic.

This does not mean denial of difficulty or indifference to suffering. It means trusting that history is not spinning out of control. Christ sustains what He created. To live as His disciple today is to anchor our confidence not in circumstances, governments, or personal security, but in the risen Lord who holds all things together.

Third, Paul reminds us that Christ's supremacy is not distant or abstract, but **personally redemptive**. This supreme Christ is also the one who has reconciled us to God through His physical body on the cross (Colossians 1:21–22). Discipleship today must never drift into admiration without gratitude.

Before we were reconciled, we were alienated from God and hostile in our minds. Paul does not soften that diagnosis. He wants us to remember what grace has done.

To live faithfully now is to live as people who know they have been brought near, forgiven, and restored at great cost. Gratitude, humility, and worship flow naturally from this remembrance.

Fourth, this passage challenges us to live as **reconciled people who pursue holiness**. Paul's goal is clear: that believers might be presented "holy in His sight, without blemish and free from accusation." (Colossians 1:22). This is not a call to perfectionism, but it is a call to seriousness. Discipleship is not merely about being forgiven; it is about being transformed, day-by-day, into the image of Christ.

To live as followers of Christ today means refusing to settle into patterns of sin under the banner of grace. Grace does not excuse sin; it breaks sin's power. Holiness is not an optional extra for advanced believers. It is the direction of every reconciled life.

Fifth, Paul calls us to live with **enduring faith rather than drifting belief**. The reconciliation Christ has accomplished is to be held fast as believers "continue in your faith, established and firm, and do not move from the hope held out in the gospel." (Colossians 1:23).

This speaks directly to modern pressures. Cultural voices constantly invite believers to soften convictions, redefine truth, or treat doctrine as negotiable. Paul's concern is not intellectual stubbornness, but spiritual stability. To live as disciples today is to remain rooted in the gospel we received, resisting both subtle drift and overt distortion.

Sixth, Paul reminds us that discipleship is lived within the context of **the Church**. Christ is not only supreme over creation; He is the head of the body, the Church (Colossians 1:18). To belong to Christ is to belong to His people. Individualistic Christianity is totally foreign to Paul's vision.

Discipleship today requires meaningful participation in the life of the Church – receiving teaching, offering service, practising forgiveness, and bearing one another's burdens. Christ's rule is expressed most visibly not in isolated spirituality, but in a community shaped by His grace.

Finally, this passage invites us to live with **gospel-shaped hope for the world**. Paul speaks of the gospel that "has been proclaimed to every creature under heaven." (Colossians 1:23). The supremacy of Christ fuels mission. If Christ is Lord of all, then the gospel is good news for all. Disciples today are not called merely to preserve personal faith, but to participate in God's reconciling purposes by bearing witness to Christ in word and life.

So how then shall we live? We live with Christ at the centre of everything. We live confidently in a world he sustains. We live gratefully as those who have been reconciled. We live seriously, pursuing holiness. We live steadfastly, holding fast to gospel hope. We live communally, as members of Christ's body. And we live missionally, trusting that the supreme Christ is still at work reconciling all things to himself.

This is not a small or comfortable vision of discipleship. But it is the only response that makes sense if Jesus Christ truly is who Paul declares Him to be.

2. CHRIST FORMED IN YOU
(Colossians 1:24 – 2:5)

Paul has just lifted our eyes to the majesty of Christ - the image of the invisible God, the firstborn over all creation, the head of the body, the reconciler of all things through the blood of His cross. The supremacy of Christ has been declared in breathtaking terms. But theology in Colossians never floats in abstraction. It moves immediately into life, ministry, and cost.

In Colossians 1:24–29, Paul opens a window into his own calling. He shows what it means to serve the supreme Christ. The passage bridges what he has said about Christ's greatness and what he will soon say about continuing in Christ. Before warning them about false teaching, he reminds them what true gospel ministry looks like. It is marked by suffering. It is centred on Christ. And it aims at maturity.

Rejoicing in costly service

Paul begins with words that challenge modern assumptions: "Now I rejoice in what I am suffering for you." (Colossians 1:24). He writes as a prisoner. His chains are not hypothetical. His suffering is not symbolic. He has endured opposition, hostility, and confinement because he preaches Christ. Yet he speaks of rejoicing.

This is not emotional denial. It is theological conviction. His suffering is "for you." It is connected to the growth and stability of the Church. Paul sees his hardship as participation in Christ's mission for Christ's body.

He continues, saying that he suffers "for the sake of His body, which is the Church." (Colossians 1:24). The Church is not peripheral to Christ's work. It is central. The supreme Christ who reconciles sinners now gathers them into a body. To serve Christ is to serve his Church. For Paul, ministry is not self-expression. It is self-giving. The cost does not surprise him because he understands the pattern of the cross.

The Christ he proclaims suffered for the redemption of his people. It is not strange that those who serve that Christ should experience opposition. This perspective guards the Colossians - and us - from shallow expectations. Faithfulness does not guarantee ease. Obedience does not eliminate hardship. But suffering for Christ is not meaningless. It is caught up in God's redemptive purposes.

A stewardship from God

Paul goes on: "I have become its servant by the commission God gave me to present to you the word of God in its fullness." (Colossians 1:25). He sees himself as a servant, not a religious entrepreneur. His ministry is not self-appointed. It is a commission from God. The language is that of stewardship - something entrusted, something to be delivered faithfully.

The content of that stewardship is "the word of God in its fullness." Paul does not offer fragments, speculations, or spiritual enhancements. He presents the whole counsel of God as it has now been revealed in Christ.

This is crucial in light of the pressures facing the Colossian Church. They are being tempted by teaching that promises deeper wisdom and hidden knowledge. Paul responds by insisting that the fullness has already been made known. He defines this message further: "the mystery that has been kept hidden for ages and generations, but is now disclosed to the Lord's people." (Colossians 1:26).

The word "mystery" does not mean something obscure or elite. It refers to God's long-hidden redemptive plan, now revealed. What generations longed to see has now been unveiled. God's saving purpose is no longer concealed. And what is this mystery?

Paul states it plainly: "To them God has chosen to make known among the Gentiles the glorious riches of this mystery, which is Christ in you, the hope of glory." (Colossians 1:27).

Here the heart of the gospel is revealed. Not merely Christ for you, though that is gloriously true. Not merely Christ above you, though he is supreme. But Christ in you. The hope of glory is not found in spiritual supplements or religious additions. It is found in union with Christ. The risen Lord dwells with and within his people by his Spirit. This is the riches Paul proclaims.

The content and goal of proclamation

Paul now summarises his ministry in one sweeping sentence: "He is the one we proclaim, admonishing and teaching everyone with all wisdom, so that we may present everyone fully mature in Christ." (Colossians 1:28). The centre is unmistakable: "He is the one we proclaim." Not techniques. Not philosophy. Not spiritual experiences. Christ.

The ministry involves both admonishing and teaching. There is instruction and there is correction. The gospel shapes minds and hearts. It comforts and confronts. Paul does not reduce preaching to encouragement alone, nor does he turn it into harsh rebuke. It is wise, balanced, and Christ-centred. The aim is equally clear: maturity.

The goal is not mere conversion, nor spiritual excitement, nor intellectual fascination. It is to present believers "fully mature in Christ." Maturity means stability. It means depth. It means believers who are rooted in Christ, resistant to deception, and growing in Christlikeness.

This aim directly prepares the way for what Paul will say in the next section about not being taken captive by hollow and deceptive philosophy. True fullness is not found by adding to Christ. It is found by growing up into Him.

Paul concludes this section with a confession of dependence: "To this end I strenuously contend with all the energy Christ so powerfully works in me." (Colossians 1:29). Ministry is labour. It is effort. Paul does not pretend it is effortless. He contends. He struggles. He pours himself out. Yet even that striving is not self-generated. The energy is Christ's. The power is Christ's.

The strength that sustains him comes from the very Lord he proclaims. This is the pattern of faithful gospel service. Christ proclaimed. Christ forming his people. Christ empowering his servants.

As we progress in this passage, Paul will deepen his concern for the Colossians' stability and assurance. But here in these opening verses, he has shown us the heart of authentic ministry: suffering embraced for the Church's sake, stewardship of the full gospel, proclamation of Christ alone, and a relentless pursuit of mature believers who stand firm in him.

Paul now widens the lens. Having just described his suffering, stewardship, and aim in ministry, he turns directly now to the Colossians and to neighbouring believers who have never seen him face to face. "I want you to know how hard I am contending for you and for those at Laodicea, and for all who have not met me personally." (Colossians 2:1). The language of struggle continues here. In chapter 1 the Apostle spoke of strenuously contending with Christ's energy. Here he applies that same intensity to prayerful concern. Paul is not physically present, but he is spiritually invested. His imprisonment has not diminished his labour for the Churches.

This is pastoral love at a distance. He has not met many of these believers, yet he carries them in his heart. The gospel binds people together beyond proximity. Ministry is not restricted to those we know well. It extends to all who belong to Christ. The tone here is deeply personal. Paul wants them to understand the depth of his concern. He is not writing casually. He is not correcting from a distance with indifference. He is contending for their stability. And why? What is the goal of this struggle? "My goal is that they may be encouraged in heart and united in love." (Colossians 2:2).

Encouraged in heart

Encouragement here is not mere uplift. The word carries the idea of strengthening, fortifying, steadying. Paul knows the pressures they face. False teaching does not always appear as obvious rebellion.

It quite often sounds plausible, wise, and spiritually attractive. Believers can be unsettled not only by persecution but by persuasive alternatives.

Paul longs for their hearts to be strengthened. In Scripture, the heart is the centre of thought, affection, and will. To be encouraged in heart is to be stabilised internally - not easily shaken, not easily seduced.

This reminds us that theological clarity and emotional resilience belong together. A Church can have orthodox statements yet anxious hearts. Paul prays for both truth and courage. Spiritual stability is not cold rigidity. It is settled confidence rooted in Christ.

United in love

Encouragement is paired with unity: "united in love." (Colossians 2:2). False teaching often fragments. It divides people into the enlightened and the ordinary, the advanced and the basic. It creates tiers of spirituality.

Paul's vision is different. Love binds believers together as equals under Christ. There is no inner circle with secret access to deeper realities. The mystery has been revealed to all God's people. Unity in love is not sentimental. It is doctrinally anchored. When Christ is central, believers draw closer to Him and therefore closer to one another. When Christ is displaced, unity fractures.

This is crucial for the Colossians. If they begin chasing additional spiritual experiences or elite insights, they risk weakening the very bond that strengthens them. Encouraged hearts and united love form the soil in which spiritual maturity grows.

Full assurance in understanding

Paul continues: "so that they may have the full riches of complete understanding." (Colossians 2:2). The language is deliberate. The false teachers promise deeper knowledge, fuller understanding, hidden wisdom. Paul insists that true riches are found not in secret additions but in settled comprehension of the gospel.

Notice the words: full riches. Complete understanding. Christian confidence is not shallow. It is not anti-intellectual. Paul desires believers to grasp deeply what God has revealed. Assurance grows as understanding deepens. The aim is not perpetual searching, but settled certainty.

And what is the object of this understanding? "In order that they may know the mystery of God, namely, Christ." (Colossians 2:2). Once again, everything narrows to a single name: Christ. Not Christ plus additional intermediaries. Not Christ supplemented by ritual or philosophical systems. Christ Himself is the revealed mystery. The goal of ministry is not complexity but clarity. Not spiritual elitism but shared knowledge of the Son of God.

All wisdom found in Him

Paul sharpens the point even further: "In whom are hidden all the treasures of wisdom and knowledge." (Colossians 2:3). This is a direct response to the cultural atmosphere surrounding the Colossians. The world they inhabited prized wisdom - philosophical insight, mystical access, deeper enlightenment.

Paul does not deny the value of wisdom. He relocates it. All treasures of wisdom and knowledge are found in Christ. There are no hidden reserves beyond Him. There is no spiritual vault that requires extra keys. The fullness resides in the person of Christ.

This statement safeguards the Church against restless spiritual curiosity that drifts from the centre. The pursuit of novelty is replaced by the pursuit of depth in Christ. The wisdom found in Him is not abstract theory. It is the wisdom of redemption, reconciliation, new creation, and union with the risen Lord. To truly know Christ is to possess riches beyond comparison.

Guarding against deception

Though Paul's explicit warning will come in the next verses, the concern is already clear. He wants them encouraged, united, assured, and rooted in Christ because persuasive alternatives are circulating.

He will soon say, "I tell you this so that no one may deceive you by fine-sounding arguments." (Colossians 2:4). The danger here is not crude heresy but subtle distortion. Arguments can sound refined, thoughtful, spiritually mature. The protection against such deception is not suspicion of learning but settled confidence in Christ. When believers understand that all treasures are in him, they are not easily drawn toward substitutes.

Paul's pastoral strategy is therefore profoundly positive. He does not begin by naming every error. He strengthens their grip on Christ, so they might have encouraged hearts, be united in love, and have complete understanding of Jesus Christ as the revealed mystery. All wisdom is found in Him.

Paul is keen to express his joy in their present stability and urge them toward continued firmness. But here, in these verses, we see the inner architecture of mature discipleship: confidence rooted in Christ, unity sustained by love, and wisdom centred entirely in the Son of God.

Paul now makes explicit what has really been quietly shaping his concern from the beginning. After describing his struggle for their encouragement, unity, and assurance in Christ, he writes: "I tell you this so that no one may deceive you by fine-sounding arguments." (Colossians 2:4).

The danger facing the Colossians is not crude unbelief. It is not open denial of Christ. It is persuasion. The arguments sound refined. They sound thoughtful. They likely promise deeper insight, fuller experience, greater spiritual maturity. This is precisely why Paul spends so much time lifting their eyes to Christ. The most effective protection against deception is not constant suspicion. It is settled clarity about who Christ is and what believers already possess in him.

The false teaching threatens to draw them away subtly - not by rejecting Christ outright, but by suggesting He is not sufficient on His own. Paul's concern is pastoral and protective. He does not want them captivated by ideas that seem elevated but ultimately displace Christ from the centre.

The subtle nature of deception

The phrase "fine-sounding arguments" suggests eloquence, plausibility, and even intellectual appeal. Error does not always present itself as rebellion. It more often than not presents itself as sophistication. For the Colossians, these teachings likely blended elements of Jewish observance, mystical spirituality, and philosophical speculation. They promised access to something more - more wisdom, more protection, more fullness.

But Paul has already declared that the fullness resides in Jesus Christ. All the treasures of wisdom and knowledge are in Him (Colossians 2:3). The revealed mystery Paul is talking about is Christ himself (Colossians 2:2).

When believers grasp this deeply, they are not easily swayed by the allure of additions. Deception thrives where confidence is thin. It struggles where assurance in Christ is thick. Paul therefore strengthens before he warns. He anchors before he corrects.

Present stability and Apostolic joy

He continues: "For though I am absent from you in body, I am present with you in spirit and delight to see how disciplined you are and how firm your faith in Christ is." (Colossians 2:5). There is genuine encouragement here. Paul does not assume collapse. He rejoices in what he sees.

The word translated "disciplined" suggests order, structure, stability. The Church is not chaotic. It is arranged and grounded in sound belief. Their faith is "firm." It is not drifting. It is not easily shaken. Paul's tone is important. He does not write as though everything is falling apart. He writes to protect what is already good. He delights in their firmness in Christ.

Notice that phrase carefully: faith in Christ. Not faith in systems. Not faith in traditions. Not faith in spiritual experiences. Faith in Christ. The firmness he celebrates is not stubbornness or narrowness. It is settled trust in the person and work of Jesus.

The flow of the argument

This brings the entire section - Colossians 1:24–2:5 - into clear focus. In chapter 1, Paul declared Christ supreme over creation and reconciliation. Then he showed the nature of his own ministry: suffering embraced for the Church's sake, stewardship of the revealed mystery, proclamation centred entirely on Christ, labour empowered by Christ.

In chapter 2, he revealed his struggle for their encouragement, unity, and full assurance. He defined the mystery as Christ. He located all wisdom in Him. Now he makes clear why this matters: so they will not be deceived. The logic is seamless:

If Christ is supreme … if Christ is the revealed mystery … if all treasures are in Christ … if the goal is maturity in Christ … then any teaching that suggests something beyond Christ must be resisted. The Church's strength lies not in complexity but in clarity.

Christ formed in You

There is a phrase earlier in this passage that gathers everything together: "Christ in you, the hope of glory." (Colossians 1:27). That is the heart of Paul's message. The hope of glory is not found in mystical ascent. It is not secured by ritual observance. It is not strengthened by spiritual elitism. It is found in union with Christ. Christ proclaimed. Christ trusted. Christ dwelling among his people.

This is why Paul labours. This is why he suffers. This is why he contends in prayer. This is why he warns. His aim is not novelty. It is maturity. His aim is not complexity. It is confidence. His aim is that believers stand firm in Christ, rooted in him, secure in him, satisfied in him.

Bridging forward

This prepares the way for what comes next. Paul will soon say, "So then, just as you received Christ Jesus as Lord, continue to live your lives in Him." (Colossians 2:6). The connection is unmistakable.

You received Christ. Continue in Christ. Do not move beyond Him. Do not be drawn away by persuasive additions. Our second sermon declared the supremacy of Christ. In this sermon we have seen the shape of ministry devoted to forming Christ in His people and guarding them from deception. In the next sermon will press the call to continue steadfastly in Him.

Here, at the close of this section, the message stands firm: The mystery has been revealed. The treasures are found in Him. The hope of glory is 'Christ in you.' Stand firm in Christ. And where hearts are encouraged, love is united, wisdom is centred on Him, and faith remains steady, the Church will not be easily shaken.

How then shall we live?

Colossians 1:24–2:5 presses discipleship into sharper focus than many of us expect. Paul does not merely defend doctrine. He shows us what faithful, Christ-centred living looks like when persuasive alternatives surround the Church. If Christ truly is supreme, and if all the treasures of wisdom and knowledge are found in Him, then our lives must reflect a settled confidence rather than a restless searching.

First, we are called to live with a **right understanding of suffering**. Paul rejoices in suffering "for the sake of His body, which is the Church." (Colossians 1:24). Discipleship today often falters when obedience becomes costly. We can assume something has gone wrong if faithfulness leads to inconvenience, misunderstanding, or resistance. Paul corrects this instinct. Suffering in service of Christ is not pointless. It is participation in the ongoing outworking of the gospel. To live faithfully now means refusing to measure God's favour by comfort. Instead, we entrust hardship to Him, believing that He can use even our limitations to strengthen others.

Second, we are called to live with a **clear sense of stewardship**. Paul speaks of a commission given to him "to present to you the word of God in its fullness." (Colossians 1:25). Every believer has received something from Christ – a responsibility, a sphere of influence, a calling.

Discipleship today means treating that calling as a trust, not a hobby. We are not free to reshape the gospel to suit preference or pressure. Like Paul, we are to handle God's word faithfully, refusing to dilute it or supplement it with what sounds impressive.

Third, this passage calls us to live with **Christ at the centre of our message and our maturity**. "He is the one we proclaim." (Colossians 1:28). Not Christian culture or spiritual techniques. Not moral improvement, but Christ. In a world saturated with religious options and spiritual enhancements, disciples today must resist the temptation to add to Him. Growth does not come from moving beyond Christ, but from going deeper into Him. The goal is to be "fully mature in Christ." (Colossians 1:28). Maturity is not novelty. It is stability rooted in Him.

Fourth, we are called to live with **encouraged hearts and united love**. Paul longs for believers to be "encouraged in heart and united in love." (Colossians 2:2). False teaching often isolates, elevates a few, or divides a community into spiritual tiers. Christ-centred discipleship does the opposite. It binds believers together as equals under grace. To live faithfully today means actively cultivating unity, speaking encouragement, and resisting the subtle pride that claims access to deeper or superior spirituality.

Fifth, Paul calls us to live with **settled assurance rather than perpetual searching**. He desires believers to possess "the full riches of complete understanding" found in Christ (2:2). Modern disciples can easily drift into spiritual restlessness, constantly chasing new experiences, fresh revelations, or deeper techniques. Paul insists that the mystery has been revealed. The riches are already given. All the treasures of wisdom and knowledge are in Christ (Colossians 2:3). To live faithfully is to grow in clarity about Him, not to drift beyond Him.

Sixth, this passage calls us to live with **discernment in a persuasive culture**. Paul warns that some may attempt to deceive by fine-sounding arguments (Colossians 2:4).

The danger is not obvious rebellion, but subtle addition. Disciples today face very similar pressures. Ideas can sound compassionate, sophisticated, or spiritually mature while quietly displacing Christ's sufficiency. Discernment does not mean cynicism. It means asking whether Christ remains central and sufficient. Where Christ is diminished, however subtly, something essential has been lost.

Seventh, we are called to live with **firm faith rather than fragile confidence**. Paul delights in their "firm... faith in Christ." (Colossians 2:5). Firmness is not stubbornness. It is steady trust grounded in truth. Discipleship today often prizes flexibility over conviction. Yet Paul celebrates stability. A Church that knows who Christ is and what He has done will not be easily shaken by intellectual trends or cultural shifts.

Finally, this passage invites us to live with **Christ formed in us as our hope of glory**. "Christ in you, the hope of glory." (Colossians 1:27). The Christian life is not sustained by external performance or elite knowledge. It is sustained by union with the living Christ. Our hope does not rest on spiritual achievement, but on His indwelling presence and promised glory.

So how then shall we live? We live as stewards of the gospel, not innovators of it. We endure suffering with confidence in God's purposes. We proclaim Christ and seek maturity in Him. We cultivate unity and encouragement. We rest in the sufficiency of Christ rather than chasing additions. We practise discernment amid persuasive voices. And we stand firm in faith, knowing that the hope of glory is not hidden elsewhere, but already present in Christ Himself.

This is steady, resilient discipleship – not flashy, not restless, but rooted in the One who is fully sufficient.

The appeal that closed the previous section now becomes a real call to action. What Paul has prayed for, laboured toward, and affirmed must now be embodied. The Colossians are not being invited into a new spiritual phase, but urged to live consistently with the Christ they have already received. The danger they face is not blatant unbelief, but quiet displacement - a gradual shift away from reliance on Christ toward other sources of security or meaning.

Continue in Christ as you began

The exhortation begins with deliberate simplicity. "So then, just as you received Christ Jesus as Lord, continue to live your lives in Him." (Colossians 2:6). The logic is unmistakable. The way the Christian life begins determines how it continues. There is no change of method, no upgrade in foundation. The Christ received at conversion is the Christ relied upon for growth.

Receiving Christ is described in specific terms. He was received "as Lord." This is not a sentimental acknowledgment or a vague spiritual openness. It' is a confession of authority. To receive Christ as Lord is to recognise His rightful rule over every aspect of life. Continuing in Him therefore means an ongoing posture of submission and trust. Growth is not achieved by seeking alternatives to Christ, but by living more fully in Him.

Rooted, built up, overflowing with thankfulness

This call to continue is then unfolded through a cluster of images that describe stability and growth. Believers are to be "rooted and built up in him, strengthened in the faith as you were taught." (Colossians 2:7). Each image contributes to a unified picture. Roots speak of nourishment and depth. A plant survives not because it resists storms on the surface, but because it draws life from beneath. Being rooted in Christ means drawing ongoing strength from Him rather than from surrounding cultural or religious influences.

The image of being built up adds intentionality. Growth is not random or accidental. It follows a foundation that has already been laid. Christ is not only the starting point of faith; He determines its shape and direction. Anything constructed that does not align with Jesus Christ will eventually prove unstable. Strengthening in the faith brings the focus back to teaching.

The Colossians are not urged to pursue novel doctrines, but to be strengthened in what they were already taught. Stability grows where truth is remembered, understood, and lived. Novelty may excite, but it rarely sustains. Faith becomes firm through clarity, not constant change.

This description of growth concludes with an emphasis that sets the tone for the whole exhortation. Believers are to live this way "overflowing with thankfulness." (Colossians 2:7). Gratitude is not a decorative virtue added to mature faith. It is a sign of health. Thankfulness flows naturally from confidence in grace already received. Those who believe they lack something that is essential will always struggle to be grateful. Those who know they have been given fullness in Christ can live with joy and contentment.

Do not be taken captive – Christ is enough

From this positive exhortation, Paul moves swiftly into warning. "See to it that no one takes you captive through hollow and deceptive philosophy." (Colossians 2:8). The language is intentionally strong. Deception is not merely misleading; it is enslaving. To be taken captive is to lose freedom, often without realising it. The threat is not open persecution, but subtle persuasion.

The philosophy described is hollow, empty of true substance. It promises insight but delivers bondage. Its source is not divine revelation, but "human tradition and the elemental spiritual forces of this world." (Colossians 2:8). Whether these forces are understood as cultural pressures, religious systems, or spiritual powers, the contrast is clear. They stand over against Christ rather than flowing from him.

The decisive issue is dependence. Such teaching "depends on human tradition and the elemental spiritual forces of this world rather than on Christ." (Colossians 2:8). The problem is not intellectual engagement or thoughtful reflection. The problem is misplaced trust. Whenever human ideas become foundational, captivity follows. Freedom is preserved only when Christ remains central.

This warning is grounded immediately in a profound theological declaration. "For in Christ all the fullness of the Deity lives in bodily form." (Colossians 2:9). This statement leaves no room for dilution. God's fullness is not spread across spiritual intermediaries or hidden realms. It dwells entirely in Christ. The incarnation remains central. God has not revealed Himself by pulling humanity upward toward abstraction, but by coming down in bodily reality.

This truth directly confronts any teaching that treats Christ as one step among many. There is nothing beyond fullness. There is nothing higher than God Himself. If all fullness dwells in Christ, then seeking fullness elsewhere is unnecessary and misguided.

The implication for believers follows immediately. "And in Christ you have been brought to fullness." (Colossians 2:10). What is true of Christ determines what is true of those who belong to Him. Believers are not incomplete, deficient, or waiting for something essential to be added. They have already been made full in Christ.

This fullness does not eliminate growth, obedience, or discipline. It redefines them. Growth is not about acquiring what is missing, but about living out what has already been given. Obedience becomes a response to grace, not a strategy for completion. Discipline flows from confidence, not insecurity.

Christ's authority is reaffirmed once more in Colossians 2:10 where we are reminded that He is "the head over every power and authority."

No spiritual force, human system, or religious structure stands alongside him. All are subject to His rule. This authority secures the believer's freedom. There is no rival power that can legitimately claim ultimate control over those who belong to Christ.

As this section unfolds, the central message is unmistakable. The Colossians are not being warned because they lack Christ, but because they possess Him. The danger lies not in deficiency, but in distraction. Having begun with Christ, they must continue in Him. Having received fullness, they must resist any voice that suggests otherwise. Everything that follows will press this truth further, showing how Christ's finished work reshapes identity, freedom, and daily life.

Having established that believers are already complete in Christ, Paul now clearly explains how that completeness has been achieved. He does not appeal to feelings, experiences, or spiritual progress, but to decisive acts of God that have already taken place. The freedom of the Christian life rests not on what believers are striving to become, but on what God has already done to redefine who they are.

A deeper cutting – the old self put off

The first image Paul employs reaches deep into Israel's covenant history. "In Him you were also circumcised with a circumcision not performed by human hands." (Colossians 2:11).

Circumcision was not merely a religious ritual. It marked covenant belonging, identity, and obligation. To be circumcised was to be bound to the law and to the covenantal expectations that came with it. By invoking this image, Paul addresses directly the pressure some believers were feeling to submit to Jewish practices as a pathway to spiritual fullness.

Yet the circumcision which Paul is describing is fundamentally different. It is not physical, visible, or administered by people. It is a divine act. The contrast could not be clearer.

What defines belonging to God under the new covenant is not an external mark, but an internal transformation accomplished by God Himself. This immediately removes all grounds for religious comparison or spiritual hierarchy.

This circumcision is explained as "the putting off of the sinful nature." (Colossians 2:11). The language is strong and deliberate. Something has been stripped away, removed like a garment that no longer belongs. Paul is not describing gradual moral improvement or behavioural adjustment. He is describing a decisive change of identity. The old self, once dominated by sin and rebellion, no longer defines who the believer is.

Crucially, this act is described as being done "by Christ." Transformation is not achieved through discipline, ritual, or effort. Christ Himself brings it about. Any teaching that subtly shifts the weight of spiritual change back onto human performance misunderstands the nature of salvation. God's bidding is God's enabling. That is, what God requires, God supplies. What God commands, God accomplishes.

Buried and raised with Christ

The imagery then moves from circumcision to burial. "Having been buried with him in baptism." (Colossians 2:12). Burial speaks of finality. What is buried is no longer active or influential. Baptism, then, is not presented merely as a symbolic act or public declaration. It is described as participation in Christ's death. The old life has been decisively dealt with. The believer's past no longer holds authority.

Yet burial is never the end of the Christian story. Paul immediately speaks of resurrection. Believers have also been "raised with Him through your faith in the working of God, who raised Him from the dead." (Colossians 2:12).

Resurrection life is not achieved by faith as effort, but received through faith as trust. The power at work is God's power, the same power that raised Jesus from the grave. This union with Christ is comprehensive.

His death becomes their death. His resurrection becomes their new life. The believer's story is now inseparably bound to Christ's story. Nothing external needs to be added to complete this transformation. Nothing is missing.

Made alive by grace – forgiven fully

Paul then reinforces the depth of this change by recalling their former condition. "When you were dead in your sins and in the uncircumcision of your flesh." (Colossians 2:13). Death is not metaphorical exaggeration. It describes real spiritual incapacity. Apart from Christ, there was no ability to restore a relationship with God or to respond rightly to Him.

Against that very bleak reality stands the decisive action of grace. "God made you alive with Christ." (Colossians 2:13). Life is not summoned from within. It is given from above. The initiative belongs entirely to God. Salvation is not cooperation between human potential and divine assistance. It is resurrection.

This new life is inseparable from forgiveness. Paul makes it clear that God "forgave us all our sins." (Colossians 2:13). The scope of forgiveness is complete. Nothing remains unresolved. No category of sin is excluded. Forgiveness is not partial, temporary, or conditional. It is full and final.

This matters deeply for believers who are tempted to submit to systems that trade in guilt, obligation, or perpetual uncertainty. Where forgiveness is complete, accusation loses its power. Where life has been given, death no longer defines identity. Paul wants the Colossians to understand that they are not spiritually unfinished. They have already been decisively transformed by union with Christ.

Having described the personal transformation believers have experienced in Christ, Paul now widens the lens to reveal the cosmic consequences of the cross. What God has done is not limited to internal renewal or individual forgiveness. It reaches into the realm of accusation, condemnation, and hostile powers that once held humanity in bondage.

The record of debt is cancelled

Paul introduces this truth with legal imagery. God has "cancelled the charge of our legal indebtedness, which stood against us and condemned us." (Colossians 2:14). Sin is not merely personal failure or moral weakness. It is debt. The law stands as a written record of obligation unmet and commands broken. That record does not merely accuse; it condemns.

The seriousness of this charge must not be minimised. The law does not negotiate or compromise. It demands 100% obedience and pronounces judgment when obedience fails. When this remains unresolved, this debt leaves humanity exposed and condemned. No spiritual technique or moral reform can erase what has already been written.

Nailed to the cross – no condemnation left

Yet Paul declares that this charge has been decisively dealt with. God has "taken it away, nailing it to the cross." (Colossians 2:14). The image is vivid and final. The record of debt has not been hidden, ignored, or postponed. It has been publicly displayed and decisively cancelled. The cross is the place where condemnation is exhausted.

To nail the charge to the cross is to declare that it has been fully paid. Nothing remains outstanding. No further payment can ever be demanded. Any teaching that revives condemnation as a means of motivation or control stands in direct contradiction to the cross.

Powers disarmed – Christ's public triumph

Paul then lifts the horizon further still. "And having disarmed the powers and authorities, He made a public spectacle of them." (Colossians 2:15). The cross, which appeared to be a moment of weakness and shame, is revealed as the site of decisive victory. The hostile powers that once exercised influence have been stripped of their weapons and exposed as defeated. These powers and authorities represent all forces that oppose God's reign, whether spiritual, ideological, or systemic.

Their strength lay in accusation, fear, and condemnation. Once the charge is cancelled, their power collapses. Disarmed, they are rendered ineffective.

The language Paul uses evokes the image of a triumphal procession. Christ has "triumphed over them by the cross." (Colossians 2:15). What appeared to be defeat was, in fact, conquest. What looked like humiliation was actually enthronement. The cross is not merely the means of forgiveness. It is the announcement of victory. This victory matters profoundly for believers tempted to submit to fear, ritual obligation, or spiritual intimidation. The powers that once accused, enslaved, and dominated have been publicly defeated. They may still attempt to intimidate, but they no longer possess legitimate authority.

The logic here is unmistakable. If sins have been forgiven, if debt has been cancelled, and if hostile powers have been disarmed, then captivity makes no sense. Freedom is not something believers must achieve. It is something Christ has already secured.

The call, then, is not to seek liberation elsewhere, but to live consistently with the victory which Christ has already won. The cross has not merely opened the possibility of freedom. It has established it. To return to fear, obligation, or spiritual anxiety is to live as though the triumph of Christ were incomplete. Christ is not one authority among many. He is the victorious Lord. And those who belong to Him share in that victory.

How then shall we live?

Colossians 2:6–15 confronts us with a decisive truth: the Christian life is not sustained by adding to Christ, but by continuing in Him. Paul moves from exhortation to declaration, calling believers to live out what is already true of them in Christ and to resist every pressure that would draw them back into fear, self-effort, or spiritual dependence on anything else. For disciples of Christ today, this passage reshapes how we think about growth, identity, freedom, and victory.

First, we are called to live with **consistency between beginning and continuing**. Paul's instruction is simple and searching: "So then, just as you received Christ Jesus as Lord, continue to live your lives in Him." (Colossians 2:6). The way we began is the way we must go on. We did not receive Christ by achievement, ritual, or insight, but by faith in His amazing grace.

Discipleship today falters when we start by grace and then attempt to continue by self-reliance. To live faithfully now is to keep trusting Christ as Lord, not merely as Saviour, day by day. Growth does not mean moving beyond dependence; it means deepening it.

Second, Paul calls us in Colossians 2:7, to live as people who are **rooted, built up, and established** in Christ. These images emphasise stability rather than novelty. Modern disciples often equate growth with constant change or new experiences. Paul points us instead toward depth. Roots grow downward before anything visible grows upward. To live well today is to cultivate habits that anchor us in Christ – regular engagement with Scripture, prayer shaped by truth, and participation in the life of the Church. Stability is not stagnation. It is the condition for lasting fruit.

Third, this passage urges us to live with **discernment in a persuasive world**. Paul warns against being taken captive through hollow and deceptive philosophy that depends on human tradition rather than on Christ (Colossians 2:8). Disciples today face a flood of voices offering meaning, identity, and fulfilment. Many sound wise, compassionate, or progressive, yet subtly shift trust away from Christ. To live faithfully is not to reject thinking, but to test it. Discernment asks whether an idea draws us deeper into Christ or quietly replaces Him as the only source of fullness.

Fourth, Paul calls us to live from the reality of **fullness already received**. He declares that "in Christ all the fullness of the Deity lives in bodily form, and in Christ you have been brought to fullness." (Colossians 2:9–10).

This is revolutionary for modern discipleship. Much Christian anxiety flows from the assumption that we are lacking – lacking power, knowledge, experience, or status. Paul insists otherwise. If we belong to Christ, we are not deficient. To live as disciples today means resisting spiritual insecurity and rejecting the pressure to chase additions to Christ. Our task is not to complete ourselves, but to live out the completeness we already have in Him.

Fifth, Paul teaches us to live as people who understand the **decisiveness of Christ's saving work**. Through vivid imagery, he reminds believers that they have been spiritually circumcised, buried with Christ, and raised with Him through faith (Colossians 2:11–12). These are not metaphors for gradual improvement, but declarations of decisive change. Discipleship today is weakened when believers live as though their old life still defines them. To live faithfully is to take seriously that our old self has been dealt with and that new life is now ours in Christ.

Sixth, Paul urges us to live in the freedom that comes from **forgiveness fully accomplished**. God has made us alive with Christ, "having forgiven us all our sins." (Colossians 2:13). There is no partial forgiveness here. For disciples today, this addresses both guilt and fear. Lingering shame, repeated self-condemnation, and anxiety about our standing with God, undermine faithful living. We live well when we take God at His word and allow forgiveness to shape our confidence, worship, and obedience.

Seventh, Paul calls us to live without fear of **condemnation or spiritual intimidation**. In Colossians 2:14–15, he declares that God has cancelled the charge of our legal indebtedness and disarmed the powers and authorities, triumphing over them by the cross. The forces that once accused, enslaved, or terrified us have been defeated. Disciples today often live as though hostile powers still have ultimate leverage. Paul insists that Christ's victory is complete. To live faithfully is to resist fear-driven spirituality and to stand confidently in the triumph of the cross.

Finally, this passage invites us to live with **gratitude rather than anxiety**. Paul therefore urges believers to be "overflowing with thankfulness." (Colossians 2:7). Gratitude is not a personality trait; it is a theological response. When we understand who Christ is and what He has done, thankfulness becomes the natural posture of the heart. Discipleship marked by gratitude is resilient, joyful, and steady.

So how then shall we live? We live by continuing in Christ as we began. We grow deep rather than restless. We practise discernment rather than spiritual curiosity detached from truth. We live from fullness, not lack. We take forgiveness seriously. We stand confidently in Christ's victory. And we cultivate grateful hearts shaped by the cross.

This is the freedom of discipleship Paul sets before us – not striving to become complete, but learning to live as those who already are, in Christ.

5. THE DANGER OF EMPTY RELIGION
(Colossians 2:16-23)

The victory of Jesus Christ described in the previous section has profound consequences for how believers relate to their faith. If sins have been forgiven, debt cancelled, and hostile powers disarmed, then the Christian life can no longer be governed by fear, obligation, or performance. Paul now draws out one of the most practical implications of Christ's finished work: believers must not allow others to sit in judgment over them on the basis of religious observance.

The warning is stated plainly and forcefully in Colossians 2:16, "Therefore, do not let anyone judge you by what you eat or drink, or with regard to a religious festival, a New Moon celebration or a Sabbath day." The word "therefore" anchors this command directly in what has just been declared. Because Christ has triumphed over accusation and condemnation, judgment on these grounds has lost its legitimacy.

Paul does not deny that food laws, festivals, or Sabbaths once had an important place in the life of God's people. These practices were woven deeply into Israel's covenant identity. They shaped daily rhythms, communal worship, and religious loyalty. But the issue here is not whether such practices once mattered. The issue is whether they still have authority to define spiritual standing.

The phrase "do not let anyone judge you" is crucial. Paul is not primarily addressing those who are judging, but those who are being judged. The danger is not only the false teaching, but also the misplaced submission. When believers allow others to pronounce verdicts on their spiritual legitimacy based on external observance, they quietly surrender the freedom Christ has secured.

This judgment is described in concrete terms. It concerns what believers eat or drink, and how they relate to sacred times. These are visible, measurable, and easily monitored practices.

That is precisely why they are so attractive as markers of spirituality. They offer very clear standards and immediate assessment. Yet Paul insists that such criteria no longer function as reliable indicators of faithfulness.

What is at stake here is not moral licence, but theological clarity. The Christian life is not defined by dietary restriction or certain calendar observances. Those things once pointed somewhere. Now that destination has been reached.

Shadows that have served their purpose

Paul explains why judgment on these grounds is inappropriate. "These are a shadow of the things that were to come; the reality, however, is found in Christ." (Colossians 2:17). This single sentence reshapes how the Old Testament law is understood. The practices Paul names were not meaningless. They were just shadows. A shadow is real, but it is not substantial. It has shape, but no independent existence. It points to something solid that stands behind it. Shadows are not false; they are preparatory. Their value lies in what they anticipate, not in their permanence.

Food laws taught Israel about holiness, separation, and dependence on God. Festivals rehearsed redemption, provision, and covenant faithfulness. Sabbaths embodied rest, divine sovereignty and trust. All of these were good gifts. But they were never the destination. They were designed to prepare God's people for something greater.

Paul declares in Colossians 2:17, that this greater reality has now arrived. "The reality… is found in Christ." The word translated "reality" carries the sense of substance or body. Christ is not another shadow. He is the substance to which the shadows pointed. To return to shadows after the substance has arrived is not devotion. It is regression.

This distinction is critical. Paul is not arguing that the law was wrong, but that its role has changed. What once functioned as a guide now functions as a witness. To treat it as binding again is to misunderstand its purpose.

This explains why religious judgment is so dangerous. When believers are evaluated on the basis of shadows rather than substance, attention is drawn away from Christ. That is religion - when what was meant to point to Him becomes a substitute for Him.

Religion doesn't have Christ at the centre

The danger Paul identifies is subtle because it often appears sincere. Those who judge on the basis of religious observance usually believe they are defending holiness. Yet sincerity does not guarantee accuracy. A system that elevates external practice above Christ's finished work inevitably distorts the gospel.

Religion is very attractive because it is controllable. Rules can be monitored. Calendars can be observed. Diets can be regulated. Spiritual standing becomes measurable. Yet such systems quietly reintroduce what Christ has already removed: condemnation. That is why God hates religion!

Paul's concern is pastoral as much as theological. When believers begin to assess themselves, or allow others to assess them, based on external observance, assurance erodes. Confidence in Christ is replaced by self-scrutiny. Freedom gives way to anxiety. This is why Paul does not say, "Do not judge others." He says, "Do not let anyone judge you." The Colossians are being called to resist illegitimate authority. They are not answerable to human verdicts grounded in outdated markers. Their standing is determined by Christ alone.

Christ as the measure of faithfulness

The contrast between shadow and reality clarifies the true measure of faithfulness. Faithfulness is not defined by conformity to religious patterns, but by union with Christ. The question is no longer whether someone keeps certain days or avoids certain foods. The question is whether they belong to Christ, trust in Him, and live from His sufficiency. This does not mean that discipline, rhythm, or practice are unimportant. It means they are no longer decisive.

Practices may serve faith, but they must never replace it. When practices become the basis of judgment, they cease to serve their purpose. Paul's language protects believers from both pride and despair. Those who observe religious practices more strictly are not elevated. Those who do not, are not diminished. All stand on the same ground: Christ himself.

The gospel creates a community in which spiritual standing is not negotiated through performance. It is received as a gift. This radically reshapes how believers relate to one another. Judgment gives way to gratitude. Comparison gives way to worship.

The direction of Paul's argument here is unmistakable. Christ has fulfilled what the law anticipated. The shadows have served their purpose. To allow judgment based on those shadows is to live as though Christ were not enough.

The danger of empty religion does not begin with open denial of Christ. It begins when Christ is subtly displaced as the centre. Paul calls the Colossians, and all believers, to refuse that displacement. The reality has arrived. It is found in Christ.

Religion does not only express itself through external rules and visible observances. It also takes a more subtle and seductive form. If legalism appeals to the desire for order and control, this next danger appeals to the desire for depth, experience, and spiritual distinction. Paul now turns to a form of religion that looks impressive, sounds spiritual, and promises insight beyond the ordinary Christian life, yet ultimately draws believers away from Christ rather than deeper into him.

The warning is again direct. "Do not let anyone who delights in false humility and the worship of angels disqualify you." (Colossians 2:18). The language is strong because the threat is serious. To be disqualified is not simply to be criticised or corrected. It is to be told that one does not truly belong, that one's faith is inadequate, incomplete, or inferior. This kind of spiritual pressure is deeply damaging, particularly when it comes clothed in religious language.

Paul identifies the character of this false spirituality as "false humility." True humility recognises dependence on God and gladly rests in Christ's sufficiency. False humility, by contrast, appears modest but subtly undermines the gospel. It downplays confidence in Jesus Christ while elevating special practices, experiences, or insights. It often sounds self-effacing, but its effect is to shift trust away from Christ and toward spiritual achievement.

This false humility is paired with "the worship of angels." (Colossians 2:18). The precise nature of this practice in Colossae is not fully known, but its function is clear. Angels were being treated as intermediaries, spiritual beings through whom access to God was supposedly enhanced. Rather than approaching God confidently through Christ, believers were being encouraged to approach Him indirectly, cautiously, and fearfully.

At its core, this reflects a diminished view of Christ. If angels must be invoked, consulted, or revered, then Christ's mediating work is no longer sufficient. What is presented as reverence is, in fact, retreat. The result is not deeper humility; the result is a much greater distance from God Himself.

Experiences elevated above Christ

Paul goes on to describe how this false spirituality operates. Such people "go into great detail about what they have seen; they are puffed up with idle notions by their unspiritual mind." (Colossians 2:18). Spiritual experiences are placed at the centre. Visions, revelations, and encounters become the basis of authority. What someone has seen becomes more important than what Christ has done.

This is a very dangerous shift. Experiences, by their nature, are personal and unverifiable. They resist correction and invite comparison. Once experiences become the final measure of spirituality, the community is divided into those who have seen and those who have not, those who are enlightened and those who are merely ordinary believers. Paul does not deny the reality of spiritual experience.

Scripture contains genuine visions and revelations. The issue here is not experience itself, but its elevation. When experience becomes the foundation of faith rather than the fruit of faith, it displaces Christ from the centre.

The irony Paul exposes is sharp. Those who appear humble are in fact "puffed up." Their spirituality produces pride rather than dependence. The mind behind it is described as "unspiritual," not because it lacks religious activity, but because it is disconnected from Christ. Spirituality without Christ at the centre is not deeper spirituality. It is distorted spirituality.

Losing hold of the Head

The heart of the problem is then named with devastating clarity. "They have lost connection with the head." (Colossians 2:19). This is the decisive issue. Everything else flows from this loss.

Christ, who has already been identified as the head of the body, is no longer the source of life, direction, and unity. Whatever replaces Him, no matter how impressive, cannot sustain the body. To lose hold of the head is not necessarily to reject Christ outright. It is to loosen the grip. It is to treat Christ as insufficient on His own, as someone who must be supplemented by additional mediators, practices, or experiences.

The tragedy is that in seeking something more, believers actually cut themselves off from the only source of true life. Paul contrasts this false spirituality with the true life of the Church. From Christ, the head, "the whole body, supported and held together by its ligaments and sinews, grows as God causes it to grow." (Colossians 2:19). Growth is not produced by mystical insight or elite experience. It is produced by connection to Christ.

The imagery is organic and relational. The Church is a body, not a machine. Life flows from the head to every part. Support, unity, and growth come through connection, not competition. When Christ remains central, the body grows in a way that God himself causes. Growth is not forced. It is given. This statement also redefines what genuine spiritual growth looks like.

Growth is not measured by unusual experiences, visionary claims, or spiritual bravado. It is always measured by healthy connection to Christ and loving integration within the body. Anything that fractures the body or elevates some above others has already departed from Christ's design.

Why religion is so dangerous

Religion is especially dangerous because it appeals to sincere desires. Many believers long for depth, intimacy with God, and a sense of the supernatural. False spirituality exploits those longings while quietly redirecting them away from Christ. It also thrives on comparison. Those who claim special insight or experience inevitably become spiritual benchmarks. Others feel inadequate, second-rate, or disqualified. Assurance erodes, not because Christ has failed, but because Christ has been displaced as the measure of belonging.

Paul's instruction is therefore both protective and liberating. "Do not let anyone… disqualify you." (Colossians 2:18). Believers are not to submit to verdicts grounded in experiences they have not shared or practices they have not adopted. Their qualification rests entirely in Christ.

The contrast could not be clearer. Empty religion builds hierarchies. Christ builds a body. Empty religion fragments and intimidates. Christ nourishes and unites. Empty religion promises growth but it delivers pride and insecurity. Christ supplies growth that God himself brings about.

A central warning comes into focus here. Any spirituality that diminishes Christ's centrality, however humble or impressive it may appear, is not a step forward, it is a step away. The danger of religion is not that it rejects Christ openly, but that it quietly loosens its grip on Him. True humility clings to Christ. True spirituality depends on Christ. True growth flows from Christ. To lose our hold of the head is to lose everything that gives life to the body.

The final danger Paul exposes is perhaps the most deceptive of all, because it looks disciplined, serious, and morally impressive.

Having warned against judgment based on religious observance and against spirituality built on visions and intermediaries, he now addresses how religion prides itself on restraint, severity, and self-control. It promises holiness through denial, but in reality, it cannot deliver what it advertises.

Paul begins by recalling the believer's fundamental change of status. "Since you died with Christ to the elemental spiritual forces of this world." (Colossians 2:20). This is not a call to die. It is a declaration that death has already taken place. Union with Christ means that believers have already died to the powers, principles, and systems that once governed their lives. The old regime no longer has authority.

The logic that follows is therefore pointed and searching. "Why, as though you still belonged to the world, do you submit to its rules?" (Colossians 2:20). To live under these regulations is not merely unnecessary. It is inconsistent. It is to behave as though nothing decisive has changed. Paul is not accusing the Colossians of abandoning Christ, but of living as though Christ's death had not fully redefined their relationship to the world.

The rules he cites in Colossians 2:21 are familiar and blunt. "Do not handle! Do not taste! Do not touch!" The repetition and abruptness of the commands highlight their severity. This is religion expressed as prohibition. It defines faithfulness primarily by avoidance and restriction. Everything is reduced to a list of forbidden actions.

Paul is not suggesting that self-control or discernment are unimportant. The problem lies deeper. These commands are described as referring to things "destined to perish with use." (Colossians 2:22). They focus on the temporary and the external. They concern material things that wear out, pass away, and ultimately have no lasting spiritual significance.

The deeper issue is their origin. These rules are "based on merely human commands and teachings." (Colossians 2:22). They do not arise from the gospel.

They are not grounded in Christ's finished work. They may sound spiritual, but they are human constructions. When such rules are elevated to markers of holiness, they quietly replace trust in Christ with trust in discipline.

The appearance of wisdom

In Colossians 2:23, Paul acknowledges why this kind of religion is attractive. "Such regulations indeed have an appearance of wisdom." They look serious. They project commitment. They signal self-denial and moral effort. In communities that value visible devotion, such practices can quickly become benchmarks of spirituality.

In the same verse, he identifies three qualities that make these practices especially persuasive. They promote "self-imposed worship, false humility and harsh treatment of the body." Each sounds commendable on the surface. Self-imposed worship suggests devotion freely chosen. False humility presents itself as modesty and restraint. Harsh treatment of the body appears to demonstrate seriousness about sin.

Yet Paul strips away the illusion by exposing their true character. This humility is false because it does not rest in Christ's sufficiency. This worship is self-imposed because it is not shaped by God's revelation in Christ. This bodily severity focuses attention on the self rather than on the Saviour. The tragedy is not that these practices are demanding, but that they are ineffective.

Paul delivers his verdict with clarity and restraint. "They lack any value in restraining sensual indulgence." (Colossians 2:23). For all their severity, they fail at the very point they promise success. They cannot change the heart.

Rules can restrain behaviour temporarily. They can shape habits and control environments. But they cannot deal with desire. They cannot transform the inner person. Sin is not defeated by restriction alone. It is defeated by new life in Christ.

Why religion fails

The failure of works-based religion lies in its diagnosis. It assumes that sin can be managed externally. If the body is punished, desires will diminish. If pleasures are removed, holiness will follow. Yet Scripture consistently teaches that sin flows from the heart. External severity cannot reach that depth.

This explains why ascetic systems often lead either to pride or despair. Those who keep the rules feel superior. Those who fail feel condemned. Neither outcome produces genuine holiness. Both keep the focus firmly on the self.

Paul's critique is therefore not dismissive, but deeply pastoral. He understands the longing behind these practices. Believers want to be holy. They want to overcome sin. They want lives that honour God. The tragedy is that they are being offered tools that cannot accomplish those goals. True transformation does not come through denying the body, but through belonging to Christ. It comes through union with Him, dependence on Him, and growth that God Himself causes. The power to resist sin does not arise from harsh treatment of the self, but from new life rooted in Christ's death and resurrection.

Freedom that guards holiness

Paul's concern throughout this passage has never been to weaken holiness. It has been to protect it. Empty religion fails not because it asks too much, but because it trusts the wrong things. It places confidence in rules, experiences, or discipline rather than in Christ.

The freedom Paul defends is not licence. It is gospel-shaped freedom. It is freedom from condemnation, freedom from false measures of spirituality, and freedom from systems that cannot change the heart. This freedom does not lead away from holiness. It leads to it. By reminding the Colossians that they have died with Christ, Paul calls them to live consistently with that reality. The old powers no longer rule. The old rules no longer define. The old measures of worth no longer apply. To submit to them again is not humility. It is forgetfulness.

The danger of religion now stands fully exposed. It may judge by observance, it may impress with experiences, or discipline through denial. But in every form, it shares the same flaw. It does not hold fast to Christ.

The answer to sin is not severity, but a Saviour. The path to holiness is not self-imposed worship, but shared life with Christ. Growth does not come from rules that perish with use, but from union with the one who gives life.

Paul's warning is therefore also an invitation. Do not live as though Christ were insufficient. Do not submit to systems that cannot save or sanctify. You have died with Christ. You now live in him. Hold fast to that reality and refuse every substitute that promises much but delivers nothing.

How then shall we live?

Colossians 2:16–23 addresses a perennial danger for disciples of Jesus Christ: that is the temptation to substitute visible religious performance for genuine spiritual life. Paul exposes forms of spirituality that appear rigorous, impressive, and disciplined, yet are ultimately powerless to produce true holiness. For disciples today, this passage is especially confronting, because the pull toward rule-based, appearance-driven religion remains strong, even within orthodox Christian settings.

First, Paul calls us to live in the **freedom secured by Christ, not under the tyranny of religious judgement**. "Therefore do not let anyone judge you by what you eat or drink, or with regard to a religious festival, a New Moon celebration or a Sabbath day." (Colossians 2:16). These practices were once God-given, but they were never meant to become ultimate. They were shadows pointing forward to Christ.

To live as disciples today means refusing to measure spiritual maturity by external observance. Food choices, calendars, styles of worship, or personal disciplines may have value, but they are not the measure of faithfulness. When such things become tests of spiritual legitimacy, Christ's sufficiency is always seriously undermined.

Second, this passage teaches us to live with **Christ as the substance, not merely the reference point**. Paul insists that these practices "are a shadow of the things that were to come; the reality, however, is found in Christ." (Colossians 2:17).

A shadow has no life in itself. It only exists because something real stands behind it. Discipleship today becomes distorted when believers cling to shadows after the substance has arrived. We honour Christ not by rehearsing religious forms for their own sake, but by living in active dependence on Him. Practices are meant to serve relationship, not replace it.

Third, Paul warns us to live with **discernment toward spirituality that appears humble but subtly displaces Christ**. He speaks of those who delight in false humility and the worship of angels, claiming access to visions and deeper spiritual insight (Colossians 2:18). This kind of spirituality often sounds impressive and deeply reverent. Yet Paul is uncompromising. Such people have "lost connection with the head." (Colossians 2:19). For disciples today, this is a vital warning. Not every spiritual claim, mystical experience, or advanced teaching is from God. If Christ is no longer central – if reliance shifts toward intermediaries, techniques, or secret knowledge – then however spiritual it appears, it is no longer Christian discipleship.

Fourth, Paul calls us to live as people who remain **actively connected to Christ, the head of the body**. (Colossians 2:19). Growth, he says, comes from Christ as the whole body is supported and held together. This reshapes how we think about spiritual progress. True growth does not come from stricter rules or deeper experiences detached from Christ. It comes from ongoing dependence on Him within the life of the body. Disciples today grow not by isolating themselves into elite spirituality, but by remaining connected to Christ and His people through faith, obedience, and mutual encouragement.

Fifth, Paul confronts the temptation to live by **rules that promise control but deliver frustration**. He challenges regulations such as "Do not handle! Do not taste! Do not touch!" (Colossians 2:21).

These commands feel decisive and practical. They give the impression that holiness can be managed through avoidance and restriction. Paul exposes the flaw. Such rules "are based on merely human commands and teachings." (Colossians 2:22). They may restrain behaviour temporarily, but they do not address the heart. Discipleship today must resist the illusion that external control equals inner transformation. Holiness grows from renewed desires, not merely restrained actions.

Sixth, Paul invites us to live honestly about the **limits of self-made religion**. He acknowledges that these practices "have an appearance of wisdom, with their self-imposed worship, their false humility and their harsh treatment of the body." (Colossians 2:23). The problem is not that they look foolish, but that they look wise. Yet Paul's verdict is decisive: "They lack any value in restraining sensual indulgence." (Colossians 2:23).

For disciples today, this is a searching reminder. Religious intensity is not the same as spiritual power. Effort alone cannot conquer sin. Only life in Christ can.

Seventh, this passage calls us to live with **confidence in Christ's completed work rather than fear-driven discipline**. The false teachers Paul confronts are ultimately motivated by fear – fear of impurity, fear of missing something, fear of judgement. Paul points believers back to what is already true: they have died with Christ to the elemental spiritual forces of this world (Colossians 2:20). Disciples today live faithfully not by acting as though they are still enslaved, but by trusting that Christ has already set them free.

Finally, Paul challenges us to live with **authentic holiness that flows from union with Christ**. True holiness is not achieved by starving the body or impressing others. It is produced as Christ reshapes our desires, affections, and loyalties from the inside out.

This kind of holiness is often quieter, slower, and less dramatic, but it is real. It bears fruit in love, humility, perseverance, and obedience.

So how then shall we live?

⇒ We live free from religious judgement.

⇒ We cling to Christ as the substance, not the shadow.

⇒ We practise discernment toward impressive but Christ-less spirituality.

⇒ We remain connected to Christ within His body.

⇒ We resist rule-based approaches that promise control without transformation.

⇒ We trust Christ's finished work rather than fear-driven discipline.

⇒ And we pursue holiness that grows from life in Him.

This is not a call to abandon discipline or obedience, but to anchor both firmly in Christ. Anything less may look spiritual, but it will never produce the life that only Christ can give.

4. LIVING THE RISEN LIFE
(Colossians 3:1-11)

The movement from chapter two to chapter three marks a decisive shift in Paul's emphasis, but not in theology. Paul does not abandon his argument about Christ's sufficiency. He presses it home. Having dismantled empty religion and exposed its inability to transform the heart, he now turns to the positive shape of Christian living. The question is no longer what believers must avoid in order to be spiritual, but how those who belong to Christ are to live in light of who they already are.

Paul begins not with command but with identity. "Since then, you have been raised with Christ." (Colossians 3:1). This is not a hypothetical statement. It is not an aspiration. It is a declaration of fact. Union with Christ in His resurrection has already taken place. The Christian life does not begin with effort, but with participation. Believers do not strive in order to be raised; they live because they have been raised.

This resurrection identity provides the solid foundation for everything that follows. Christian ethics are never detached from Christian theology. Note that Paul did not say, "Try to live like resurrected people." He said, in effect, "You are resurrected people – therefore now live accordingly." Behaviour flows from belonging. Practice flows from position.

A new direction for the mind

Because believers have been raised with Christ, a new orientation is required. "Set your hearts on things above, where Christ is, seated at the right hand of God." (Colossians 3:1). The heart here represents desire, allegiance, and direction. To set the heart is to fix one's loyalty. We should not think that Paul is encouraging escapism or detachment from everyday life here. He is calling us to re-centre our priorities around the risen Christ.

The reference to Christ being seated at the right hand of God is significant. This is the place of authority, victory, and completed work. Christ is not striving or struggling. He reigns.

To set the heart where Christ is, means to live under the authority of the One who has already triumphed. It is to allow His reign to shape values, decisions, and ambitions.

Paul reinforces this call by repeating it in slightly different terms. "Set your minds on things above, not on earthly things." (Colossians 3:2). Heart and mind together encompass the inner life. Desire and thought are to be redirected. Earthly things here do not simply mean material objects or physical existence. They refer to a whole way of thinking shaped by fallen priorities – self-centredness, status, control, and immediate gratification.

This reorientation is necessary because something decisive has already happened. "For you died, and your life is now hidden with Christ in God." (Colossians 3:3). Death language again appears, echoing earlier chapters. The old life has ended. The believer's true life is no longer defined by visible markers or public recognition. It is hidden.

To be hidden with Christ does not mean obscure or insignificant. It means secure. Hidden life is protected life. It is a life anchored in God's keeping rather than in human approval. This directly confronts the insecurity that fuels so much empty religion. When life is hidden with Christ, it no longer needs to be displayed, defended, or proven.

The hope of future glory

Paul now lifts the horizon beyond the present. "When Christ, who is your life, appears, then you also will appear with Him in glory." (Colossians 3:4). This statement gathers past, present, and future into one sentence. Christ is not merely the giver of life. He is life itself. Identity is not found in achievements, experiences, or disciplines, but in relationship with him.

The future appearance of Christ brings with it the promise of shared glory. What is now hidden will one day be revealed. The tension of the Christian life lies here. Believers already belong to the risen Christ, yet they live in a world that does not yet reflect that reality. Hope sustains faith in the present by anchoring it in God's promised future.

This future perspective is not speculative or escapist. It provides motivation for holiness now. Because believers will appear with Christ in glory, they are called to live in a way that reflects that destiny. Paul does not threaten with judgment here. He motivates with hope.

Putting to death the old way of life

Paul now moves to explicit commands. "Put to death, therefore, whatever belongs to your earthly nature." (Colossians 3:5). The word "therefore" matters. This call flows from resurrection identity, not from any fear of punishment. Holiness is not an attempt to earn life. It is the expression of life which has already been given.

The language of putting to death is deliberately strong. Sin is not to be managed, negotiated with, or tolerated. It is to be killed. Paul lists behaviours that were common in the surrounding culture and remain powerfully relevant. Sexual immorality, impurity, lust, evil desires, and greed are named plainly, with greed identified as idolatry (Colossians 3:5). Desire that claims ultimate loyalty becomes a rival god.

Paul does not minimise the seriousness of these sins. He connects them to divine judgment. "Because of these, the wrath of God is coming." (Colossians 3:6). This is not a threat aimed at believers, but a reminder of the destructive reality of sin. These behaviours belong to the old-world order that stands under judgment. They are incompatible with life in Christ.

The reminder in Colossians 3:7 is a personal one: "You used to walk in these ways; in the life you once lived." Paul does not shame the Colossians. He reminds them of change. This is no longer who they are. The call to holiness is grounded in transformation, not denial of the past.

A new identity, a new community

Paul then widens the scope beyond private behaviour to relational life. Anger, rage, malice, slander, and filthy language are to be put away (Colossians 3:8).

These sins fracture community and contradict the new identity believers share. Speech, in particular, reveals the heart. A resurrected life cannot be marked by destructive words.

Truthfulness therefore becomes essential. "Do not lie to each other, since you have taken off your old self with its practices" (Colossians 3:9). Deception belongs to the old life. The new life is characterised by honesty because it is grounded in truth.

Paul now returns once more to identity. Believers have "put on the new self, which is being renewed in knowledge in the image of its Creator." (Colossians 3:10). Renewal is ongoing, but its direction is also very clear. It restores what sin distorted. The image of God, once marred, is being renewed through union with Christ.

The call to live the risen life does not remain at the level of inward orientation alone. Having redirected the heart and mind toward Christ and named the decisive break with the old life, Paul now presses the implications into the daily patterns of behaviour and community life. Resurrection is not merely a doctrine to be affirmed. It is a reality that must reshape conduct, speech, and relationships.

The language Paul uses in Colossians 3:5 is deliberately forceful. "Put to death, therefore, whatever belongs to your earthly nature." This is not a suggestion for gradual improvement or moderation. It is a call for decisive action. Sin is not something to be managed politely. It's something to be killed. The strength of the language matches the seriousness of the issue.

Paul lists behaviours that belong to the old order of life. Sexual immorality, impurity, lust, evil desires, and greed are named plainly (Colossians 3:5). These are not arbitrary moral prohibitions. They are expressions of a life curved inward on itself. Desire becomes destructive when it seeks ultimate satisfaction apart from God. Greed is singled out and named for what it truly is: idolatry. When desire claims ultimate loyalty, it becomes a rival god.

This exposure of idolatry is crucial. Sin is not merely about breaking rules. It is about misplaced worship. The old life is governed by desires that promise fulfilment but deliver bondage. The risen life calls believers to recognise these desires for what they are and to refuse their authority.

Paul connects these behaviours to divine judgment. "Because of these, the wrath of God is coming." (Colossians 3:6). This statement is not meant to terrify believers into obedience. It is meant to clarify reality. These patterns of life belong to a world that stands under judgment. They are incompatible with the new creation inaugurated in Christ. To cling to them is to live out of step with the future God has secured.

The reminder that follows is personal and pastoral. "You used to walk in these ways, in the life you once lived." (Colossians 3:7). Paul does not deny the past. He names it. But he names it as past. This is no longer who they are. The call to holiness is not grounded in shame, but in transformation. The Colossians are not being asked to pretend they were never sinners. They are being reminded that they are no longer defined by sin.

Putting off the old patterns

Paul now turns from desires to dispositions. "But now you must also rid yourselves of all such things as these: anger, rage, malice, slander, and filthy language from your lips." (Colossians 3:8). These sins disrupt relationships and fracture community. They reveal hearts still shaped by the old order of hostility and self-protection.

Anger and rage describe unchecked emotional responses that erupt destructively. Malice reveals settled ill-will toward others. Slander and abusive speech demonstrate how deeply sin corrupts communication. Words, which were created to give life, are twisted into weapons.

A risen life cannot be marked by speech that destroys rather than builds. Paul adds a specific command that strikes at the very heart of trust within the community. "Do not lie to each other." (Colossians 3:9).

Deception belongs to the old life. It thrives where fear and self-interest dominate. The new life, by contrast, is characterised by truthfulness because it is grounded in God's truth. The reason for this call is again rooted in identity. Believers have "taken off your old self with its practices." (Colossians 3:9). The imagery is that of clothing. The old self is not something to be tailored or repaired. It is something to be removed. The practices that once flowed naturally from that old identity no longer fit. This removal is paired with a positive reality. Believers have "put on the new self, which is being renewed in knowledge in the image of its Creator." (Colossians 3:10).

The new life is not static. It is being renewed. Growth is ongoing, but its direction is clear. Renewal moves believers toward the image of God, the very image that sin distorted and Christ restores. This renewal is not merely behavioural. It is relational and cognitive. It involves growing knowledge of God, not merely information about him. To know God truly is to be reshaped by that knowledge. The risen life is marked by increasing alignment between who God is and who his people are becoming.

A new humanity in Christ

Paul now draws out one of the most radical implications of resurrection life. "Here there is no Gentile or Jew, circumcised or uncircumcised, barbarian, Scythian, slave or free, but Christ is all, and is in all." (Colossians 3:11). The old categories that once defined worth, status, and belonging have been rendered obsolete.

These distinctions were deeply entrenched in the ancient world. Ethnic identity, cultural background, religious status, and social rank determined one's place in society. Paul does not deny that these distinctions exist. He denies that they have any authority in defining identity within the people of God. The word "here" is decisive.

In the realm created by resurrection life, the old hierarchies lose their power. Belonging is no longer negotiated through background or achievement. It is grounded entirely in Christ.

This does not erase diversity. It reorders it. Differences remain, but they no longer function as barriers or measures of worth. Christ becomes the defining reality. He is all, and he is in all. Identity is no longer fragmented. It is unified in him.

This vision of a new humanity guards against two dangers at once. It resists pride by stripping away grounds for superiority. It resists despair by removing grounds for exclusion. No one stands above others, and no one stands outside. All who belong to Christ share equally in his life.

Living the risen life together

The risen life Paul describes is not an individual achievement. It is a shared reality. Sin disrupts community. Resurrection restores it. As believers put to death what belongs to the old life and put on the new self, the church becomes a living demonstration of God's new creation.

This transformation is not instantaneous, but it is real. Renewal is ongoing. Struggle remains. Yet the direction is unmistakable. The old life is being stripped away. The new life is being formed. Christ is shaping a people who reflect his character and share his life.

Paul's vision is demanding, but it is also deeply hopeful. He does not call believers to become something they are not. He calls them to live out what they already are in Christ. Resurrection life is not an unreachable ideal. It is the present reality of those who belong to the risen Lord. The shape of that life will be filled out even further.

What begins with death to the old self and renewal into a new humanity will be expressed in compassion, love, peace, and gratitude. But everything rests on this foundation: you have been raised with Christ. Live as those who belong to him.

The risen life Paul describes is not an abstract ideal or a spiritual aspiration reserved for the few. It is the concrete, everyday reality of those who belong to Christ.

Having established the believer's new orientation toward Christ, the decisive break with the old life, and the formation of a new humanity, Paul now brings these themes together to show how resurrection life reshapes both personal identity and communal existence.

At the heart of this passage stands a radical claim: the believer's true life is no longer anchored in what is visible, measurable, or immediately affirmed. "For you died, and your life is now hidden with Christ in God." (Colossians 3:3). This hiddenness does not imply insignificance or uncertainty. It speaks of security. The believer's life is bound up with Christ himself and kept by God. What defines the Christian most truly is not open to public scrutiny or human evaluation.

This hidden life explains why the Christian experience can at times be marked by tension. There is a disconnect between who believers really are and how the world perceives them. The surrounding culture continues to evaluate worth according to status, achievement, power, or visibility. Resurrection life operates on an entirely different basis. Its centre is unseen, its source is Christ, and its security rests in God's keeping rather than human approval.

Living between hiddenness and glory

Paul does not allow this hiddenness to collapse into passivity or resignation. He immediately anchors it in hope. "When Christ, who is your life, appears, then you also will appear with him in glory." (Colossians 3:4). Hiddenness is not permanent. What is presently concealed will one day be revealed. The Christian life moves toward manifestation, not obscurity.

This future appearance gives meaning to present obedience. Holiness is not pursued to gain glory, but because glory is assured. The believer's destiny is already bound to Christ's destiny. As surely as Christ will appear, those who belong to him will share in that appearing. This promise sustains faithfulness when obedience is costly and when the world's values clash with the way of Christ.

The phrase "Christ, who is your life" is especially significant. Christ is not merely an influence on life or an addition to it. He is life itself. Identity is no longer constructed from personal history, cultural background, or moral performance. It is defined relationally. To belong to Christ is to have one's life redefined at its deepest level.

The seriousness of sin in the risen life

It is precisely because resurrection life is real that sin must be treated seriously. Paul's call to "put to death" what belongs to the earthly nature is not harsh moralism. It is spiritual realism. Sin is incompatible with the life believers now possess. It does not merely contradict Christian ethics; it contradicts Christian identity.

The list of sins Paul names is not exhaustive, but representative. Sexual immorality, impurity, lust, evil desires, greed, anger, rage, malice, slander, abusive speech, and deceit all belong to the old order of existence (Colossians 3:5–9). These behaviours thrive where self reigns supreme and where desire is allowed to define truth. They fracture relationships, distort worship, and undermine community.

Paul's insistence on putting these things to death reminds believers that grace does not make sin harmless. Forgiveness does not turn sin into a minor inconvenience. Sin remains destructive, even for those who are forgiven. The risen life therefore involves vigilance, not complacency. Yet this vigilance is not driven by fear. It is driven by clarity. The Colossians are reminded that this is who they once were, not who they are now. "You used to walk in these ways, in the life you once lived." (Colossians 3:7). The language of "used to" matters. The past is acknowledged, but it no longer defines the present.

Clothing the new self

Paul's imagery of taking off and putting on captures the practical outworking of resurrection life. The old self has been removed. The new self has been put on. This new self "is being renewed in knowledge in the image of its Creator." (Colossians 3:10).

Renewal is ongoing. Resurrection life is not static perfection, but progressive transformation. This renewal involves growing alignment with God's character. Knowledge here is not mere information.

It is relational knowing that reshapes perception, desire, and behaviour. As believers come to know God more truly, they are increasingly reshaped into his likeness. The image of God, distorted by sin, is being restored through union with Christ. This means that growth is not self-directed or self-generated. Renewal is something God is doing. Believers participate through obedience, but the power and direction of change come from God. This guards against both pride and despair. Growth is real, but it is God's work. Failure is not final, but neither is sin trivial.

A community shaped by resurrection

Paul now draws together the communal implications of this new life. "Here there is no Gentile or Jew, circumcised or uncircumcised, barbarian, Scythian, slave or free, but Christ is all, and is in all." (Colossians 3:11). Resurrection life does not merely change individuals. It creates a new kind of community.

The categories Paul lists represent some of the deepest divisions of the ancient world. Ethnicity, religion, culture, and social status defined who belonged and who did not. These distinctions carried real power and real consequences. Paul does not deny their existence. He denies their authority. In the realm created by resurrection life, these distinctions no longer function as measures of worth or belonging. Christ becomes the defining reality. He is "all" in the sense that he is the supreme measure of identity, and he is "in all" in the sense that every believer shares equally in his life.

This vision dismantles both superiority and exclusion. No one may claim higher standing on the basis of background, culture, or status. No one may be marginalised or dismissed for lacking them. Resurrection life produces a community where identity is shared, not competed for.

This does not erase difference. It redeems it. Diversity remains, but hierarchy collapses. Unity is not achieved by sameness, but by shared belonging to Christ.

Living what is already true

Paul's exhortation throughout this passage rests on a single conviction: the Christian life flows from what is already true. Believers are not asked to manufacture resurrection life. They are called to live consistently with it. They are not striving to become God's people. They are learning to live as those who already are.

This guards against two equal and opposite errors. One is legalism, which treats obedience as a means of earning life. The other is complacency, which treats grace as permission to ignore transformation. Paul rejects both. Resurrection life is given freely, and it reshapes everything.

The shape of the risen life now stands clearly before us. It is a life hidden with Christ, sustained by hope, serious about sin, marked by renewal, and expressed in a transformed community. It is not an elite spirituality or an unreachable ideal. It is the normal Christian life, grounded in union with the risen Lord.

The call is therefore simple, but profound. Since you have been raised with Christ, live as those whose life is found in him. Strip away what no longer belongs. Put on what reflects your new identity. And let Christ, who is your life, define who you are and how you live.

How then shall we live?

Colossians 3:1–11 marks a decisive turning point in the letter. Paul moves from exposing false paths to describing the true shape of the Christian life. Because believers have been raised with Christ, their lives are now to be re-oriented around a new reality. Discipleship is not about improving the old self, but about living out a new identity already given in Christ. For those seeking to follow Jesus today, this passage speaks directly to our priorities, our inner lives, and our daily choices.

First, Paul calls us to live with **a reoriented focus**. "Since, then, you have been raised with Christ, set your hearts on things above." (Colossians 3:1). This is not an invitation to escapism or disengagement from the world. It is a call to allow heaven's values to shape earthly living. Disciples today are constantly pressured to define success, happiness, and identity by what is immediate and visible. Paul insists that our deepest orientation must be upward – toward Christ, who is seated at the right hand of God. To live faithfully now is to ask not merely, *What do I want?* but *What reflects the reign of Christ?*

Second, Paul presses us to live with **renewed thinking, not merely altered behaviour**. "Set your minds on things above, not on earthly things." (Colossians 3:2). Transformation begins in the mind – in what we dwell on, desire, and value. Much modern discipleship focuses on behaviour management while leaving thought patterns largely untouched. Paul reverses this. To live as disciples today means intentionally shaping our thinking through Scripture, prayer, and reflection on who Christ is. What fills our minds will inevitably shape our lives.

Third, Paul reminds us to live from the truth of **a hidden but secure identity**. "For you died, and your life is now hidden with Christ in God." (Colossians 3:3). This statement challenges our obsession with visibility, recognition, and validation. In Christ, our truest life is hidden – secure, protected, and not dependent on public approval. Disciples today often live anxiously, driven by the need to prove themselves. Paul invites us instead to rest in the security of belonging to Christ. We live not to construct an identity, but to express one already given.

Fourth, Paul lifts our eyes to live in light of **future glory**. "When Christ, who is your life, appears, then you also will appear with him in glory." (Colossians 3:4). This future certainty reshapes present obedience. Discipleship today often struggles because we expect immediate payoff for faithfulness. Paul reminds us that the Christian life is lived between resurrection and glory. Faithfulness now may go unnoticed, but it is not wasted. Our future with Christ gives weight and meaning to present obedience.

Fifth, Paul calls us to live with **decisive seriousness about sin**. "Put to death, therefore, whatever belongs to your earthly nature." (Colossians 3:5). The language is strong and intentional. Paul does not call for gradual tolerance or negotiated compromise with sin. He calls for decisive action.

For disciples today, this challenges casual attitudes toward patterns of behaviour that contradict new life in Christ. Sexual immorality, impurity, lust, evil desires, and greed are not dismissed as personal weaknesses. They are named as realities that belong to the old life and must not be allowed to rule the new.

Sixth, Paul insists that disciples live with **clarity about what no longer defines them**. He reminds believers that these practices once characterised their lives, but no longer do (Colossians 3:7). Discipleship today requires honesty about the past without being imprisoned by it. We neither deny who we were nor allow it to determine who we are becoming. Grace enables real change. To continue living as though the old self still reigns is to forget what Christ has done.

Seventh, Paul broadens the call to include **relational transformation**. Anger, rage, malice, slander, filthy language, and deceit are to be put away (Colossians 3:8–9). These sins often feel more socially acceptable than others, yet they are just as destructive to Christian community.

Disciples today must recognise that holiness is not only about private morality, but about how we speak, react, and treat one another. A risen-life faith produces changed relationships.

Eighth, Paul grounds all of this in the reality of **new creation identity**. Believers have "put on the new self, which is being renewed in knowledge in the image of its Creator." (3:10). This renewal is ongoing.

Discipleship is not instant perfection, but continual formation. God is actively reshaping his people to reflect Christ more clearly. Growth may be slow, but it is real.

Finally, Paul calls us to live with **gospel-shaped equality and unity**. In Christ, old dividing lines lose their defining power. "Here there is no Gentile or Jew, circumcised or uncircumcised, barbarian, Scythian, slave or free, but Christ is all, and is in all." (Colossians 3:11). Discipleship today must confront divisions of culture, status, and identity that threaten unity. Our deepest identity is not found in background or social position, but in Christ alone.

So how then shall we live? We live with hearts and minds oriented toward Christ. We rest in a secure, hidden identity. We take sin seriously without despair. We pursue transformed relationships. We live patiently between resurrection and glory. And we allow Christ to redefine who we are and how we belong to one another.

This is the risen life Paul sets before us – not a life of anxious striving, but a life increasingly shaped by the reality that we have been raised with Christ, and that our true life is found in him.

Having called believers to put to death what belongs to the old life, Paul now turns to what must replace it. The Christian life is never merely about removal; it is about renewal. It is not enough to cast off sinful patterns if nothing takes their place. The life that has been raised with Christ must now be visibly expressed, and Paul directs our attention to the relational life of the church. These verses show us what happens when Christ is not only believed in but allowed to shape a people from within.

A grace-given identity that shapes conduct

Before Paul gives a single exhortation, he anchors everything in identity. "Therefore, as God's chosen people, holy and dearly loved…" (Colossians 3:12). This is not decorative language. It is foundational. The Colossians are reminded that their position before God is not the result of their effort, but of His grace. They are chosen, not because they proved themselves worthy, but because God set His love upon them. They are holy, not because they have achieved moral perfection, but because they now belong to Him. They are dearly loved, not tolerated or merely accepted, but embraced with deep and enduring affection.

Paul begins here because everything that follows must grow out of this reality. If this identity is forgotten, the commands will feel heavy and artificial. But when it is remembered, obedience becomes the natural expression of a life already secured in Christ.

It is from this position of grace that Paul calls them to action: "clothe yourselves…" (Colossians 3:12). The imagery is both simple and profound. Just as clothing is something deliberately put on and something visible to others, so these qualities are to be consciously embraced and clearly seen. The Christian life is not hidden in abstraction. It takes shape in attitudes, responses, and relationships. What Paul now describes is nothing less than the character of Christ reflected in his people.

The character of a Christ-shaped people

He speaks of compassion, kindness, humility, gentleness, and patience. Each of these qualities moves outward toward others. Compassion is a heart that is not indifferent but responsive, willing to feel the weight of another person's struggle. Kindness gives that compassion form, expressing care in ways that are practical and often unnoticed. Humility resists the instinct to elevate oneself and instead recognises that all we have is received. Gentleness is strength that does not need to assert itself harshly, but is controlled and measured, even under pressure. Patience endures over time, refusing to become irritated or withdrawn when others fail or disappoint.

These are not natural dispositions for most people, nor are they personality traits reserved for a few. They are the outworking of a life being shaped by Christ. Where Christ is central, these qualities begin to take root. Paul's concern is not merely individual transformation, but the life of the community as a whole. These virtues are not cultivated in isolation. They are formed in the friction and fellowship of real relationships. This is why he immediately continues, "Bear with each other..." (Colossians 3:13).

The exhortation assumes that life together will involve difficulty. People will misunderstand one another. They will act unwisely, speak carelessly, or fall short in ways that strain relationships. The church is not a gathering of finished people, but of those who are being renewed. To bear with one another is to remain committed in that reality. It is the refusal to withdraw or to quietly distance oneself when relationships become demanding. It is a deliberate choice to stay, to endure, and to allow space for growth, just as God has done with us.

Patience and forgiveness in real community

This leads naturally to the heart of Paul's instruction: forgiveness. "Forgive one another if any of you has a grievance against someone." (Colossians 3:13). Paul does not treat forgiveness as an occasional necessity, but as an expected pattern of life.

Grievances will arise; that is not in question. The question is how they will be handled. And here Paul gives the standard that governs everything: "Forgive as the Lord forgave you." (Colossians 3:13). The measure of our forgiveness is not the severity of the offence or the response of the other person, but the grace we ourselves have received. The forgiveness given in Christ was not partial, reluctant, or conditional. It was complete, costly, and freely given. To forgive in this way is to release the debt, to refuse to hold the offence as something to be repaid, and to allow grace to reshape the relationship.

This is not easy. It cuts against our natural instincts for self-protection and fairness. Yet it is essential. Without forgiveness, resentment takes root, relationships fracture, and the unity of the church is quietly undermined. With forgiveness, the gospel becomes visible. The community begins to reflect the grace it proclaims. What Christ has done is not only remembered; it is reenacted in the life of His people.

In these verses, Paul is not describing an idealised community that exists only in theory. He is describing what must become real wherever Jesus Christ is truly at the centre. A people secure in their identity, clothed in Christlike character, committed to one another in patience, and marked by forgiveness that flows from the cross. This is the beginning of a community shaped not by preference or personality, but by the transforming presence of Christ himself.

Having established the character that must mark the people of God, Paul now draws those qualities together under a single governing reality. Compassion, kindness, humility, gentleness, and patience are not meant to exist in isolation. They are to be held together, shaped, and completed by something greater. Without this, even the best virtues can become strained, inconsistent, or incomplete.

Love as the bond of perfect unity

Paul therefore writes in Colossians 3:14, "And over all these virtues put on love, which binds them all together in perfect unity."

Love is not presented as an additional quality alongside the others, but as the one that gives them coherence. It is the bond that holds everything in place.

Without love, compassion can become selective, kindness can become mechanical, and patience can become reluctant. Love gives warmth, direction, and authenticity to every other virtue. It ensures that what is expressed outwardly is rooted inwardly in genuine care.

This love is not merely emotional or instinctive. It is shaped by the love believers have already received. Paul has already described them as "dearly loved" (Colossians 3:12), and it is that divine love which now becomes the overall pattern for their relationships. They are not called to generate something new, but to reflect what has already been given.

This is why love produces unity. It binds believers together, not by erasing differences, but by holding them in a shared commitment to one another. Unity in the Church is not achieved through uniformity of personality or opinion, but through love that is rooted in Christ.

The peace of Christ as the ruling authority

Paul now moves from what binds the body together to what governs its inner life. "Let the peace of Christ rule in your hearts, since as members of one body you were called to peace." (Colossians 3:15). The language here suggests authority. The peace of Christ is to act as the ruling influence, the deciding voice in the life of the believer and the community.

This peace is not simply a feeling of calm. It is the peace established through Christ's reconciling work. Earlier in the letter, Paul has spoken of the peace made "through His blood, shed on the cross." (Colossians 1:20). That objective reality now becomes the basis for how believers relate to one another. When tensions arise, and they will, the question is no longer driven by personal preference or self-justification.

Instead, the peace Christ has established becomes the standard. What reflects that peace? What honours the reconciliation already achieved? To "let" this peace rule implies that believers must actively yield to it. It does not impose itself automatically. There is a decision involved, a willingness to allow Christ's work to shape our responses rather than our instincts.

Called to one body – marked by thankfulness

Paul reinforces this by reminding them of their shared identity: "since as members of one body you were called to peace." (Colossians 3:15). They do not exist as independent individuals. They belong to one another. The health of the body depends on the relationships between its members.

Division, therefore, is not a minor issue. It is a contradiction of what the church is. If Christ has reconciled them to God, that reconciliation must now be reflected in how they treat one another.

Paul then adds a brief but very important exhortation: "And be thankful." (Colossians 3:15). This is not a minor addition. Thankfulness shapes the tone of the Christian life. It guards against complaint, entitlement, and quiet dissatisfaction. A thankful heart recognises grace. It remembers what has been given rather than focusing on what is lacking. In a community marked by gratitude, relationships are softened, patience is strengthened, and unity is protected. Where thankfulness is absent, tension grows easily. Where thankfulness is present, grace is continually recognised.

Paul now brings the life of the Christian community to its fullest expression. Having shown the character that must be worn and the love and peace that must govern relationships, Paul now reveals what must dwell at the centre of the church's life and what must shape everything it does. These final verses gather the whole of discipleship into a unified vision: a people formed by the word of Christ, expressing that formation in worship, and carrying it into every part of life.

The Word of Christ dwelling richly

Paul writes, "Let the message of Christ dwell among you richly…" (Colossians 3:16). The language is deliberate and expansive. The word of Christ is not to visit occasionally or be consulted when convenient. It is to dwell, to take up residence, to become a settled and shaping presence within the community. This is more than familiarity with Scripture. It is saturation. The message of Christ is to permeate the thinking, speaking, and life of God's people. It is not confined to public teaching but shared among believers as they speak to one another.

Paul continues, "as you teach and admonish one another with all wisdom…" (Colossians 3:16). The responsibility for spiritual growth is not placed on a few individuals alone. It belongs to the whole community. Believers are to instruct one another, to encourage one another, and when necessary, to correct one another.

This mutual ministry requires wisdom. It is not harsh or careless. It is thoughtful, measured, and shaped by the truth of Christ. The word does its work not only from the pulpit, but in the shared life of the church. When the word of Christ dwells richly, the community is strengthened. Believers are less vulnerable to error, more stable in their faith, and more capable of encouraging one another.

Worship flowing from grateful hearts

Paul then shows how this word-filled life expresses itself: "through psalms, hymns, and songs from the Spirit, singing to God with gratitude in your hearts." (Colossians 3:16). Worship is not presented as performance or formality. It is the natural overflow of hearts shaped by the word and filled with gratitude. The variety of expressions – psalms, hymns, and spiritual songs – suggests richness and diversity, but the focus remains clear: worship directed to God. The key phrase is "with gratitude in your hearts." Worship is not sustained by style, preference, or atmosphere. It is sustained by thankfulness. Where gratitude is present, worship becomes genuine.

Where gratitude fades, worship becomes routine. This connects directly to what Paul has already said. A community marked by love and governed by peace will also be a community marked by thankful worship. The vertical and horizontal dimensions of the Christian life are inseparable. As believers sing, they are not only expressing praise, but they are also reinforcing truth. Worship becomes a means of teaching, reminding, and strengthening one another in the faith.

Christ at the centre of everything

Paul concludes with a statement that gathers the entire passage into a single, comprehensive call: "And whatever you do, whether in word or deed, do it all in the name of the Lord Jesus, giving thanks to God the Father through Him." (Colossians 3:17).

There is no area of life left untouched. "Whatever you do" extends beyond Church gatherings, beyond explicitly religious activity, into every word spoken and every action taken. The Christian life is not divided into sacred and secular.

All of life falls under the lordship of Christ. To do something "in the name of the Lord Jesus" is to act under his authority and for His honour. It means that our speech, our decisions, our relationships, and our responsibilities are all shaped by our allegiance to Him.

This brings coherence to the entire passage. The character described in verse 12, the forgiveness required in verse 13, the love that binds in verse 14, the peace that rules in verse 15, and the word that dwells in verse 16 all find their ultimate expression here. Christ is not an addition to life. He is the centre of it.

Paul again includes the note of thankfulness: "giving thanks to God the Father through him." (Colossians 3:17). Gratitude is not occasional. It is woven into everything. It frames both worship and daily living. Where thankfulness is present, obedience becomes joyful rather than burdensome. Where Christ is central, life becomes unified rather than fragmented.

In these verses, Paul presents a complete picture of a Christ-centred community. A people shaped by the word, expressing their faith in worship, and living every aspect of life under the lordship of Christ with grateful hearts. This is not a narrow vision. It is an all-encompassing one. Christ dwelling, Christ shaping, Christ ruling, Christ being honoured in everything. And where this becomes reality, the Church is not only instructed by the gospel. It becomes a living expression of it.

How then shall we live?

Colossians 3:12–17 moves discipleship firmly into the realm of daily relationships, attitudes, and shared life. Having called believers to put off the old self, Paul now calls them to *put on* a new way of living that reflects who they already are in Christ. This passage is deeply practical, yet it is grounded entirely in grace.

Paul does not tell believers to become something they are not; he tells them to live in line with what God has already made them. For disciples of Christ today, this text reshapes how we understand character, community, worship, and peace.

First, Paul calls us to live from a **grace-defined identity rather than self-generated virtue**. He addresses believers as "God's chosen people, holy and dearly loved" (Colossians 3:12). This identity comes before any command. Modern discipleship often reverses this order, urging people to behave better in order to belong more fully. Paul insists on the opposite. We clothe ourselves with compassion, kindness, humility, gentleness, and patience *because* we are chosen, holy, and loved. To live faithfully today means returning again and again to this identity, especially when we are tempted to define ourselves by failure, comparison, or performance.

Second, Paul teaches us to live with **deliberate, chosen character**. The virtues he reminds us to "put on" are not personality traits reserved for the naturally gentle or patient. They are Christlike qualities that believers are called to practise intentionally. Discipleship today involves conscious formation.

We do not drift into compassion or humility. We choose them, often against our instincts. To live well is to ask, in concrete situations, what it looks like to respond with Christlike restraint, empathy, and kindness rather than defensiveness or self-assertion.

Third, Paul urges us to live with **forgiveness as a defining habit**, not a rare exception. "Bear with each other and forgive one another if any of you has a grievance against someone." (Colossians 3:13). The Church is assumed to be a place where grievances arise. Paul is realistic about community life. What distinguishes Christian discipleship is not the absence of conflict, but the presence of forgiveness. Forgiveness is grounded not in the worthiness of the other person, but in the pattern set by Christ: "Forgive as the Lord forgave you." (Colossians 3:13). Disciples today must resist both bitterness and avoidance. Forgiveness is not weakness; it is obedience shaped by grace.

Fourth, Paul calls us to live with **love as the unifying centre of Christian life**. "Over all these virtues put on love, which binds them all together in perfect unity." (Colossians 3:14). Love is not one virtue among many; it is the bond that holds them together. Without love, patience becomes endurance without warmth, humility becomes self-effacement, and gentleness becomes passivity. Discipleship today must guard against virtue without love – behaviour that looks correct but lacks generosity of heart. Love gives coherence and credibility to Christian character.

Fifth, Paul teaches us to live under the **rule of Christ's peace**. "Let the peace of Christ rule in your hearts, since as members of one body you were called to peace." (Colossians 3:15). Peace here is not simply inner calm. It is relational harmony shaped by Christ's reconciling work. The word "rule" suggests an umpire or decision-maker.

Disciples today are called to allow Christ's peace to guide how conflicts are resolved, how differences are navigated, and how unity is preserved. This challenges reactive, defensive, or combative approaches to disagreement within the Church.

Sixth, Paul calls us to live as people **formed and governed by the word of Christ**. "Let the message of Christ dwell among you richly." (Colossians 3:16). Scripture is not meant to skim the surface of Church life. It is meant to take up residence. Disciples today grow shallow when Scripture is marginalised or treated as optional. Paul envisions a community shaped by teaching, admonishing, wisdom, and worship that flows from God's word. This involves both receiving and speaking the truth to one another with humility and care.

Seventh, Paul integrates discipleship with **worship that engages the whole life**. Singing psalms, hymns, and spiritual songs is not presented as performance, but as a response of gratitude (Colossians 3:16). Worship flows from hearts shaped by grace. This reminds us that worship is not confined to a service or style. It is an expression of a thankful life rooted in Christ. Gratitude fuels worship, and worship reinforces gratitude.

Finally, Paul calls us to live with **Christ-centred intentionality in everything**. "Whatever you do, whether in word or deed, do it all in the name of the Lord Jesus." (Colossians 3:17). This is the most comprehensive vision of discipleship possible. There is no neutral space. Speech, actions, relationships, and responsibilities are all to be carried out under Christ's authority and for his honour. Discipleship today is not about religious moments added to ordinary life. It is about ordinary life lived consciously in the presence of Christ.

So how then shall we live? We live from our identity as loved and chosen people. We intentionally clothe ourselves with Christlike character. We practise forgiveness as a settled way of life. We allow love to bind our community together. We let Christ's peace govern our relationships. We allow his word to dwell richly among us. We worship with gratitude. And we seek to honour Christ in everything we say and do. This is not a call to moral perfection; it is a call to Christ-shaped community. It is the daily, ordinary outworking of a life which is hidden with Christ and now expressed through love, peace, and grateful obedience.

The lordship of Christ does not remain abstract or confined to gathered worship. Paul now brings the transforming power of the gospel into the most ordinary and formative spaces of human life. Having described a community shaped by love, peace, gratitude, and the word of Christ, he turns deliberately to the household. The Christian faith is not proven first in public ministry, but in daily relationships where character is tested and shaped. Paul's instructions here are often called a "household code," yet they are unlike anything found in the surrounding Greco-Roman world. Ancient household structures were rigidly hierarchical and overwhelmingly shaped by power. Authority flowed downward, and submission was expected without qualification. Paul does not abolish structure, but he radically reshapes it by placing every relationship under the lordship of Christ.

"In the Lord" is the key phrase that governs this entire section and is implicit rather than repeated. Every command assumes Christ's authority, Christ's example, and Christ's transforming presence. The household is no longer a space which is governed by social convention alone. It becomes a place of discipleship.

Wives and the shape of Christlike submission

Paul begins with wives in Colossians 3:18. "Wives, submit yourselves to your husbands, as is fitting in the Lord." This instruction has often been misunderstood, misapplied, and misused. It must be read carefully, within its gospel framework, and under Christ's authority. The call to submission is not grounded in cultural superiority or male dominance. It is grounded in what is "fitting in the Lord."

That phrase is decisive. Submission here is not blind obedience or enforced silence. It is a willing orientation of respect and partnership shaped by allegiance to Christ. Paul does not say wives are inferior, passive, or less spiritual.

Throughout this letter, believers share equally in Christ, equally in resurrection life, and equally in the image of God. Submission, then, is not about value. It is about order within a redeemed relationship.

Importantly, Paul addresses wives directly. In the ancient world, household instructions were typically given only to male heads of households. By speaking directly to wives, Paul affirms their moral agency and spiritual responsibility. They are addressed as disciples of Christ, not as property or dependents. Submission "in the Lord" also sets clear limits. Anything that contradicts Christ's character, Christ's teaching, or Christ's lordship cannot be justified by this command. The authority of Christ always stands above every human relationship.

Husbands and the call to Christlike love

Paul's instruction to husbands is equally radical. "Husbands, love your wives and do not be harsh with them." (Colossians 3:19). In the ancient world, husbands were rarely commanded to love. Authority was assumed. Paul reshapes that assumption entirely. Love here is not defined by sentiment or dominance. It is defined by Christ. To love as a husband is to reflect Christ's self-giving, sacrificial care.

This love seeks the good of the other, even at personal cost. It rejects cruelty, manipulation, and emotional distance. The prohibition against harshness is telling. Harshness includes verbal cruelty, emotional coldness, intimidation, and misuse of authority. Paul recognises how easily power can corrupt even within intimate relationships. The gospel confronts that corruption directly.

Christ's lordship does not reinforce domination. It actually transforms authority into service. A husband's leadership is not exercised through control, but through love that builds, protects, and honours. This is not weakness. It is strength which is shaped by grace. Together, these instructions redefine marriage. It becomes neither a contest for control nor a rigid hierarchy, but a relationship shaped by mutual devotion to Christ. Submission and love are not opposing forces. They work together.

Children and the formation of obedience

Paul then addresses children directly. "Children, obey your parents in everything, for this pleases the Lord." (Colossians 3:20). Once again, the direct address matters. Children are treated as participants in the Christian community, capable of responding to Christ's authority. Obedience here is framed not merely as family order, but as an act that pleases the Lord. The child's relationship to Christ is not postponed until adulthood. Even within the family, discipleship is already taking shape.

This obedience is comprehensive but not absolute. The phrase "in everything" must be read in harmony with the Lord's authority. Obedience that requires sin or contradicts Christ's will, cannot be demanded. Yet within the normal patterns of family life, obedience forms humility, trust, and responsibility. Paul assumes that parents are exercising authority under Christ. Children are not obeying arbitrary power. They are learning to live under authority that reflects God's care and wisdom.

Fathers and the responsibility of nurture

Paul now speaks specifically to fathers in Colossians 3:21, "Fathers, do not embitter your children, or they will become discouraged." In the ancient household, fathers held nearly absolute power. Paul addresses that power directly and restrains it. The danger Paul names is discouragement. Children can be crushed not only by physical severity, but by constant criticism, unrealistic expectations, emotional neglect, or inconsistent discipline. Authority exercised without tenderness will never produce true obedience. It produces resentment or despair.

Paul's concern here is pastoral and deeply realistic. Children who are embittered lose heart. They withdraw, rebel, or internalise failure. The gospel reshapes parental authority so that it nurtures rather than wounds. This instruction implies patience, consistency, and compassion. Fathers are called not merely to command, but to cultivate. Parenting becomes a form of discipleship in which children are guided toward Christ, not driven into fear.

Again, Christ stands at the centre. Parents exercise authority as those who themselves live under authority. They model repentance, grace, and faithfulness. The home becomes a place where the character of Christ is learned long before it is articulated.

The household under Christ's Lordship

As this section closes, the pattern becomes clear. Paul is not offering cultural advice or reinforcing social norms. He is showing what happens when Christ's lordship enters the household. Marriage is reshaped by love and respect rather than power. Parenting is shaped by nurture rather than control. Children are formed in obedience that honours Christ. Authority is transformed, not abolished. This is not idealistic or naïve. Paul assumes real families, real tensions, and real failures. Yet he insists that Christ's resurrection life reaches into these spaces. The gospel is not only believed. It is lived at home. The household becomes the proving ground of faith. Where Christ reigns here, his reign becomes visible everywhere else.

Paul now turns from the relationships within the immediate family to those shaped by work and authority. In doing so, he brings the lordship of Christ into one of the most demanding and morally complex areas of everyday life. Faith is not suspended when believers enter the workplace. It is tested there. The gospel does not bypass structures of power and obligation. It confronts them and reshapes how believers live within them.

Paul begins by addressing those with the least social power. "Slaves, obey your earthly masters in everything." (Colossians 3:22). This instruction must be read carefully and responsibly. Paul is not endorsing slavery as a moral good, nor is he sanctifying injustice. He is speaking into a social reality that already existed and showing how allegiance to Christ transforms life within broken systems.

What matters immediately is that Paul addresses slaves directly. They are not spoken about; they are spoken to. This alone is radical in its context.

Slaves are treated as moral agents, capable of obedience that honours Christ. Their lives matter to God, and their faithfulness is seen by him. Paul qualifies the obedience he calls for. It is not to be superficial or driven by fear. "Not only when their eye is on you and to curry their favour." (Colossians 3:22). The temptation Paul exposes is familiar in every age. It is the temptation to work only when observed, to shape effort around approval rather than integrity.

The gospel confronts this temptation by redirecting motivation. Believers are to obey "with sincerity of heart and reverence for the Lord." (Colossians 3:22). The true audience of their work is not the earthly master, but Christ himself. Reverence for the Lord transforms obedience from mere compliance into an act of worship.

Work reoriented by Christ's Lordship

Paul now expands this principle beyond slavery to encompass all forms of labour. "Whatever you do, work at it with all your heart, as working for the Lord, not for human masters." (Colossians 3:23). With these words, work itself is redefined. Work is no longer merely a transaction of effort for reward. It becomes service rendered to Christ. This does not make work easier, but it makes it meaningful. Even unseen, repetitive, or unjustly rewarded labour is dignified when it is offered to the Lord.

The phrase "whatever you do" removes all hierarchy of tasks. There is no division between sacred and secular labour. No work is spiritually neutral. The issue is not the nature of the task, but the allegiance of the worker. When Christ is Lord, even ordinary work becomes an arena of discipleship.

This perspective guards against resentment and despair. Those trapped in difficult or demeaning circumstances are reminded that their labour is not wasted. Christ sees. Christ values. Christ receives their work as service to himself. Paul grounds this call in hope. "Since you know that you will receive an inheritance from the Lord as a reward." (Colossians 3:24).

This promise is extraordinary given the audience. Slaves, who possessed no legal right to inheritance, are assured of one from God himself. Earthly systems deny them security. God does not. The reward Paul speaks of is not payment for productivity. It is inheritance. It flows from belonging. Those who belong to Christ are heirs, regardless of their present status. This future certainty sustains present faithfulness.

Then in Colossians 3:24, Paul names the true master of every believer. "It is the Lord Christ you are serving." This declaration relativises every human authority. Earthly masters may exercise real power, but they do not possess ultimate authority. Christ does.

This truth does not excuse injustice or minimise suffering. It anchors obedience in something deeper than circumstance. Believers are not defined by their role. They are defined by their relationship to Christ.

Justice without partiality

Paul closes this section with a sober reminder that applies to all. "Anyone who does wrong will be repaid for their wrongs, and there is no favouritism." (Colossians 3:25). Christ's lordship includes accountability. Grace does not nullify justice. This statement cuts both ways. Those under authority are reminded that wrongdoing matters.

Obedience to Christ never includes sin. Those in authority are warned that power does not protect them from judgment. Christ shows no partiality. Status, position, and privilege carry no weight before Him.

For those who suffer injustice, this is a word of assurance. Wrong is seen. Wrong is named. Wrong will not be ignored forever. Believers are not called to vengeance, but to trust the righteous judgment of Christ. For those who exercise authority, this is a word of restraint. Power is not absolute. Authority is always accountable. Leadership under Christ must reflect his justice and His care.

Faith lived in ordinary labour

Paul's teaching here brings the gospel into the rhythm of ordinary work. Faith is not confined to worship gatherings or spiritual practices. It is lived out in effort, obedience, integrity, and perseverance. Work becomes a sphere where character is revealed and formed. Serving Christ reshapes motivation. Hope reshapes endurance. Accountability reshapes authority. The lordship of Christ does not remove believers from broken systems overnight. It gives them a way to live faithfully within them while looking toward a future where justice is complete and authority is redeemed.

Therefore, the reach of Christ's reign becomes unmistakable. He is Lord of the household. He is Lord of the workplace. He is Lord over those who obey and those who command. Nothing lies outside his claim. And nothing offered to him in faith is ever wasted.

Paul now addresses the final group within the household and workplace structure: those who hold authority. With a single, very carefully worded sentence, he brings balance, restraint, and gospel accountability to every exercise of power. What has been said to wives, husbands, children, and slaves now presses upward to those who command. Christ's lordship does not bypass authority. It judges it, reshapes it, and places it under a higher rule. The instruction is brief but weighty. "Masters, provide your slaves with what is right and fair, because you know that you also have a Master in heaven." (Colossians 4:1). In one sentence, Paul dismantles the assumption that authority is absolute and redefines leadership as stewardship under Christ.

Authority reframed under Christ

In the ancient world, masters were accustomed to near-total control. The law favoured them. Social structures reinforced their dominance. Paul does not deny the existence of authority, but he radically limits it. Masters are not ultimate. They answer to someone higher. The command is not vague.

Masters are to provide what is "right and fair." These are moral categories, not merely legal ones. What is lawful in society is not always what is right before God. Christ's lordship introduces a higher standard that transcends cultural norms. To act rightly is to act in accordance with God's character. To act fairly is to treat others with justice and equity. Paul does not allow masters to hide behind custom, convenience, or power. Authority must now be exercised consciously under Christ's gaze. This is a significant shift. Leadership is no longer defined by what one is permitted to do, but by what one ought to do in light of Christ's authority. Power is not abolished, but it is morally constrained.

A shared accountability before God

Paul grounds this command in a theological reality that strips authority of arrogance. Masters are to act justly "because you know that you also have a Master in heaven." (Colossians 4:1). This reminder levels the ground completely. Earthly distinctions do not disappear, but they are relativised. Masters and slaves alike stand under the authority of Christ. The one who commands answers to the One who reigns. No position exempts anyone from accountability.

This truth reshapes how power is understood. Authority becomes derivative rather than intrinsic. It is borrowed, not owned. It is exercised on behalf of Christ, not in competition with him. Paul does not threaten explicitly here. He does something more effective. He reminds masters that Christ sees, Christ judges, and Christ reigns. Leadership lived with this awareness becomes humbler, gentler, and more just.

The Gospel's quiet subversion of power

Paul's approach here is subtle but profound. He does not call for revolt. He does not incite rebellion. He does something more enduring. He plants gospel truth at the heart of authority structures, where it begins to work from the inside out. When masters understand themselves as servants of Christ, exploitation becomes harder to justify. When leaders know they answer to Christ, cruelty becomes inconsistent with faith.

The gospel quietly undermines systems of domination by redefining what leadership is for. This does not mean Paul is indifferent to injustice. It means rather that he recognises the transformation rooted in Christ's lordship reaches deeper than external reform alone. Changed hearts reshape behaviour. Renewed allegiance reshapes authority. This verse anticipates what the New Testament continues to affirm elsewhere: leadership in Christ's kingdom is always accountable, always restrained, and always shaped by justice and care.

Christ as the measure of leadership

Paul's instruction forces a question that every person with authority must face. How does Christ's lordship shape the way power is exercised? Whether in households, workplaces, Churches, or communities, authority is always a test of faith. To provide what is right and fair requires attentiveness, self-restraint, and moral courage. It requires listening to those with less power. It requires refusing to exploit vulnerability. It requires recognising that leadership exists for the good of others, not merely for efficiency or control.

This vision challenges modern assumptions as much as ancient ones. Authority today may wear different clothing, but the temptations remain the same. Power still seeks self-protection. Status still tempts entitlement. Paul's words confront these tendencies with quiet force. Christ's lordship does not eliminate authority. It redeems it.

The household and workplace under One Lord

With this final instruction, the entire household and workplace code comes into clear focus. Every relationship has now been addressed. Wives and husbands, children and parents, slaves and masters all stand under the same Lord. No group is ignored. No group is absolute. Everyone answers to Christ.

This is the unifying truth of the passage. The Christian household and workplace are not defined by who holds power, but by who reigns. Christ stands above every relationship as Lord, judge, and example.

This truth prevents despair among those with little power and restrains arrogance among those with much. It affirms dignity without encouraging disorder. It sustains obedience without legitimising abuse. The gospel does not flatten relationships into sameness. It orders them under Christ.

Living faithfully under Christ's Lordship

Paul's teaching here brings the reach of the gospel into sharp focus. Faith is not confined to belief or worship. It is lived out in authority exercised rightly, obedience offered sincerely, and relationships shaped by justice and love.

Christ's lordship extends into kitchens and workshops, offices and homes, places of command and places of service. No sphere is neutral. No role is spiritually insignificant. For those who lead, this passage calls for humility and justice. For those who serve, it offers dignity and hope. For the whole community, it declares that Christ reigns over all.

The central truth in this part of Paul's teaching stands clear. Christ is Lord of the Church, the household, and the workplace. He governs how authority is exercised and how obedience is offered. He sees what is hidden and judges without favouritism. To live under his lordship is not to escape responsibility. It is to live with greater seriousness, deeper hope, and clearer purpose. Where Christ rules, relationships are transformed. Where Christ is acknowledged as Master, power is restrained, service is dignified, and faith becomes visible in everyday life.

How then shall we live?

Colossians 3:18–4:1 brings discipleship into some of the most ordinary and demanding spaces of life: marriage, family, and work. Paul shows that following Christ is not confined to Church gatherings or private spirituality. It is worked out in kitchens and living rooms, in conversations between parents and children, and in workplaces shaped by authority, responsibility, and power. For disciples of Christ today, this passage challenges us to see everyday relationships as arenas of obedience shaped by the lordship of Christ.

First, Paul calls us to live with **Christ at the centre of our closest relationships**. Instructions to wives and husbands in Colossians 3:18, are not grounded in cultural convention, but in belonging "in the Lord." Marriage, in Paul's vision, is not a contest for control but a shared submission to Christ. For modern disciples, this reframes marriage away from self-fulfilment as the ultimate goal. Love, respect, and mutual responsibility are expressions of obedience to Christ, not merely emotional preference. To live faithfully today means asking not, *What do I want from this relationship?* but, *How does my conduct reflect Christ's lordship here?*

Second, Paul challenges husbands to live with **sacrificial love rather than relational dominance**. "Husbands, love your wives and do not be harsh with them." (Colossians 3:19). Authority, where it exists, is never permission for cruelty, neglect, or emotional withdrawal. Love here is active, protective, and costly. For disciples today, this confronts any form of relational behaviour that wounds rather than nurtures. Christlike love seeks the good of the other, even at personal cost.

Third, Paul calls families to live with **obedience shaped by care and wisdom**. Children are instructed to obey, while fathers are warned not to embitter or discourage their children (Colossians 3:20–21). This balance is crucial. Authority without compassion produces resentment, not faithfulness. For disciples today, parenting becomes a form of discipleship itself. Children are not merely to be controlled, but shepherded. Discipline aims at formation, not domination. Encouragement strengthens faith far more effectively than intimidation.

Fourth, Paul extends discipleship decisively into the realm of **work and authority**. Slaves are instructed to obey earthly masters sincerely, not merely when watched, but "with sincerity of heart and reverence for the Lord." (Colossians 3:22). While the social structures differ today, the principle remains deeply relevant. Work is not spiritually neutral. Discipleship shapes how believers approach responsibility, integrity, and effort. To live faithfully today means working not merely for human approval, but as those who serve Christ himself.

Fifth, Paul seeks to reframe work by grounding it in **eternal significance**. "Whatever you do, work at it with all your heart, as working for the Lord, not for human masters." (3:23). This transforms mundane tasks into acts of worship. Disciples today often struggle with frustration or boredom in work. Paul reminds us that Christ sees faithfulness even when others do not. Our labour is not wasted when it is offered to him.

Sixth, Paul introduces a strong word about **accountability and justice**. God shows no favouritism (Colossians 3:25). This applies to both those under authority and those who exercise it. Disciples today must resist the temptation to justify unfair treatment, exploitation, or abuse of power. Christian obedience never excuses injustice. Instead, it exposes it. The instruction to masters makes this explicit. "Provide your slaves with what is right and fair, because you know that you also have a Master in heaven." (Colossians 4:1). Authority is relativised by accountability to Christ. For modern disciples in leadership, management, or influence, this is searching. Power is to be exercised with fairness, restraint, and awareness that all authority is temporary and answerable to Christ.

Finally, this passage calls us to live with **integrated discipleship**, not divided lives. Paul does not separate "spiritual" obedience from everyday conduct. Marriage, parenting, and work all fall under Christ's rule. Discipleship today often falters when faith is confined to certain spaces while other areas remain untouched. Paul insists that Christ's lordship reaches into all of life.

So how then shall we live? We live with Christ shaping our closest relationships. We practise love that protects rather than harms. We parent with encouragement as well as authority. We work with integrity and wholeheartedness. We resist injustice and abuse of power. And we remember that in every role we occupy, we serve under the gaze of Christ. This vision dignifies ordinary life. It assures disciples today that faithfulness in unseen places matters deeply. Where Christ rules our homes and our work, the gospel becomes visible, and everyday obedience becomes an act of worship.

As the Apostle Paul begins the final part of his letter, he turns from the ordering of relationships within the household and workplace to the outward posture of the Church in the world. What he addresses now is not secondary or optional. Prayer and witness belong at the heart of Christian life together. A community shaped by Christ's lordship must also be a community shaped by dependence on God and attentiveness to those beyond its walls.

Paul begins with a command that is simple in form but demanding in practice. "Devote yourselves to prayer, being watchful and thankful." (Colossians 4:2). Prayer is not presented here as a momentary activity or an occasional response to crisis. It is to be a settled pattern of life. Devotion implies persistence, priority, and intentional commitment. Prayer is not squeezed into the margins of life. It is given space at the centre. This call to devotion recognises a fundamental truth about the Christian life. Believers do not sustain themselves by insight, effort, or discipline alone. They live in constant dependence on God. Prayer is the practical expression of that dependence. A Church that prays acknowledges that it cannot generate fruit by its own strength.

Watchfulness in prayer

Paul then adds a crucial qualifier to this devotion. Believers are called to be "watchful." (Colossians 4:2). Watchfulness implies alertness and awareness. Prayer should never be mechanical or inattentive. It requires discernment. To be watchful in prayer is to remain awake to God's activity, to spiritual danger, and to the needs of others. This watchfulness has biblical resonance.

Throughout Scripture, God's people are warned against spiritual drowsiness. Distraction, complacency, and self-sufficiency dull spiritual sensitivity. Prayer that is watchful resists these dangers. It keeps the Church attentive to what God is doing and to where obedience is required.

Watchful prayer also recognises opposition. Paul has already spoken of powers and authorities that resist God's work. Prayer is not merely reflective. It is engaged. It stands alert in a world where faithfulness is contested and where perseverance is required. This kind of watchfulness is not anxious vigilance. It is grounded attentiveness shaped by trust. Believers watch not because they fear God's absence, but because they expect his activity. Prayer keeps the Church oriented toward God's purposes rather than absorbed by its own concerns.

Thankfulness as the atmosphere of prayer

Alongside watchfulness, Paul highlights thankfulness. Believers are to pray while being "thankful." (Colossians 4:2). Gratitude is not an optional tone. It is the atmosphere in which Christian prayer is meant to be offered. This emphasis on thankfulness echoes earlier sections of the letter. Gratitude flows naturally from confidence in Christ's sufficiency. Those who know they have been forgiven, reconciled, and made alive with Christ are freed from anxious striving. Prayer becomes response rather than demand.

Thankfulness guards prayer from becoming self-centred or transactional. It reorients attention away from what is lacking and toward what has been given. In doing so, it cultivates humility and joy. A thankful Church prays with open hands rather than clenched fists.

Gratitude also sustains perseverance in prayer. When answers seem delayed or circumstances remain difficult, thankfulness anchors faith in God's past faithfulness. Prayer shaped by gratitude does not depend entirely on immediate outcomes. It rests in God's character.

Prayer for the advance of the gospel

Paul now turns from general instruction to a specific request. He does not ask first for relief from hardship or comfort in difficulty. He asks for the gospel to advance. "And pray for us, too, that God may open a door for our message." (Colossians 4:3).

Even as an apostle, Paul does not treat prayer as a formality. He depends on the prayers of the Church. The image of an open door is significant. Doors are opened by God, not forced by human ingenuity. The spread of the gospel is not finally a matter of strategy or opportunity alone. It is a matter of divine action. Paul recognises that only God can create genuine openings for his word.

This request also reveals Paul's understanding of mission. He does not see himself as a lone agent carrying the gospel forward independently. He sees the Church as participating through prayer. Those who remain in Colossae share in the work of those who travel and speak. Prayer binds the Church together in a shared calling.

In Colossians 4:3, Paul clarifies the content of the message he longs to proclaim. It is "the mystery of Christ, for which I am in chains." The mystery once hidden and now revealed remains central. The gospel Paul proclaims is not a general religious message. It is the announcement of Christ himself. The mention of chains is striking. Paul does not ask the Colossians to pray primarily for his release. He asks them to pray for opportunity. His circumstances do not determine his priorities. Even imprisonment is viewed through the lens of witness. Paul's concern is not self-preservation, but faithfulness.

This challenges many common assumptions about effectiveness. Doors can be opened even when circumstances appear restrictive. God's mission is not hindered by confinement or limitation. Paul's chains become the context for the gospel's advance rather than its obstruction.

Clarity in proclamation

Paul adds a further request that sharpens the focus. "Pray that I may proclaim it clearly, as I should." (Colossians 4:4). Opportunity alone is not enough. Clarity matters. The gospel must be spoken plainly and faithfully. This request reflects humility. Paul does not assume that his gifting or experience guarantees clarity.

He recognises the need for God's help even in proclamation. Clear speech is a gift to be sought, not a skill to be presumed. Clarity also reflects responsibility. The gospel is not to be obscured by unnecessary complexity, fear, or compromise. To proclaim Christ clearly is to present Him faithfully, without distortion or dilution. Paul is conscious that the message entrusted to him carries eternal weight. This concern for clarity reinforces the seriousness of Christian witness. The Church does not merely speak about Christ. It bears responsibility for how Christ is represented. Prayer undergirds that responsibility by acknowledging dependence on God's enabling.

Prayer as participation in mission

Taken together, these verses reshape how prayer is understood. Prayer is not retreat from action. It is participation in God's mission. Through prayer, the Church joins in the work of opening doors, sustaining witnesses, and advancing the gospel. Paul's requests also reveal the proper ordering of concerns. Personal comfort, safety, and resolution of hardship are not ignored, but they are not primary. The advance of the gospel takes precedence. Prayer aligns the Church's desires with God's purposes.

This does not diminish the reality of suffering or difficulty. It reframes them. When prayer is devoted, watchful, and thankful, hardship becomes context rather than obstacle. God's purposes are pursued even in limitation.

The pattern is clear in this passage - a Church that lives wisely in the world must first be a Church that prays. Watchful prayer guards against complacency. Thankful prayer guards against fear. Missional prayer aligns the Church with God's work beyond itself.

Paul's call is therefore both demanding and hopeful. Devote yourselves to prayer. Stay awake. Give thanks. Pray for open doors. Pray for clear proclamation. In doing so, the Church participates actively in God's unfolding work, confident that he who opened the mystery of Christ will also open doors for its announcement.

Prayer, as Paul has shown, shapes the inner life of the Church and aligns it with God's mission. But prayer does not replace action. It prepares for it. Having called the Colossians to devoted, watchful, thankful prayer, Paul now turns to how that praying community is to live visibly and wisely among those who do not yet share their faith. The movement is deliberate: dependence on God flows into discernment in the world.

Paul's instruction is concise but far-reaching. "Be wise in the way you act toward outsiders; make the most of every opportunity." (Colossians 4:5). The term "outsiders" is not dismissive or hostile. It is descriptive. It refers to those outside the believing community, those who observe Christian life before they ever hear a Christian explanation. Paul assumes that the Church is always being watched, whether consciously or unconsciously.

Wisdom as a way of life

The call to wisdom echoes themes already present throughout the letter. Wisdom is not secret knowledge or elite insight. It is the ability to live rightly in light of who Christ is. To act wisely toward outsiders is to live in a way that reflects Christ's character and honours His lordship in ordinary interactions.

Wisdom here is practical and relational. It involves discernment about behaviour, priorities, and responses. It recognises that not every situation is the same and not every moment carries the same weight. Wise living requires attentiveness, restraint, and intentionality.

Paul does not call for withdrawal from the world or aggressive confrontation with it. He calls for thoughtful engagement. The Christian life is not to be hidden away, but neither is it to be reckless. Wisdom navigates between fear and presumption.

This wisdom is especially important because Christian conduct can either clarify or confuse the gospel. Behaviour that contradicts the message undermines it. Behaviour shaped by grace adorns it. Paul understands that how believers live often speaks before what they say.

Making the most of every opportunity

Paul adds urgency to this call. Believers are to "make the most of every opportunity." (Colossians 4:5). The phrase carries the sense of redeeming time, of recognising moments that matter and refusing to waste them. Opportunities for witness are not endless or automatic. They must be recognised and stewarded. This does not mean forcing conversations or manufacturing encounters. It means living with attentiveness to God's providence. Doors open and close. Moments arise unexpectedly. Wise believers are alert to these moments and ready to respond.

The connection to prayer is crucial. A praying Church becomes an attentive Church. Those who ask God to open doors are more likely to recognise when doors open. Prayer sharpens perception. It trains believers to see their lives not as random sequences of events, but as contexts for faithful witness. Paul's emphasis here also counters passivity. Faith is not meant to be private or inert. It moves outward. Wisdom does not lead to silence. It leads to readiness.

Speech that reflects grace

Paul now turns from conduct in general to speech in particular. "Let your conversation be always full of grace, seasoned with salt." (Colossians 4:6). Words really matter. They can carry weight. They can shape impressions. Paul does not restrict this instruction to formal evangelism. It applies to everyday conversation. Speech "full of grace" reflects the gospel itself. Grace is unearned. Gracious speech is marked by patience, generosity, and respect. It avoids harshness, superiority, and defensiveness. It does not seek to win arguments at the expense of people.

Grace-filled speech does not mean evasive or vague speech. It means truthful speech shaped by love. Grace does not dilute truth. It carries it with care. Paul adds another metaphor: speech seasoned with salt. Salt in the ancient world preserved and enhanced flavour. Speech seasoned with salt is neither bland nor corrosive. It has substance. It engages interest. It brings clarity without bitterness.

Salted speech avoids extremes. It is not dull or timid, but neither is it abrasive or careless. It reflects thoughtful engagement with others, shaped by awareness of context and sensitivity to the hearer. This image suggests that Christian speech should be attractive without being manipulative, clear without being cruel, and confident without being arrogant. Such speech reflects wisdom at work.

Answering each person appropriately

Paul now states in verse 6, the purpose of this gracious, seasoned speech. "So that you may know how to answer everyone." The emphasis is not on memorised formulas or rehearsed scripts. It is on discernment. Different people require different responses. Questions arise from different places. Objections carry different emotional weight. Wise witness always listens before it speaks. It seeks to understand before it responds.

This instruction guards against treating people as projects. Outsiders are not problems to be solved. They are people to be engaged. Paul's vision of witness is personal not mechanical. This also places responsibility on believers to be thoughtful about their faith. Knowing how to answer requires reflection, learning, and humility. It involves growing understanding of the gospel and sensitivity to human experience.

At the same time, this responsibility is not meant to intimidate. Paul has already rooted everything in prayer. Believers are not left to rely on their own cleverness. God opens doors. God grants clarity. God shapes wisdom. Faithful witness flows from dependence, not self-confidence.

Witness as a way of being

What emerges from these verses is a vision of witness that is integrated rather than isolated. Witness is not an occasional activity added to Christian life. It is the natural overflow of a life shaped by prayer, wisdom, and grace. Conduct and speech belong together. Wise living creates credibility. Gracious speech provides explanation.

Opportunities are not seized through pressure, but through presence. The Church's life becomes a context in which the gospel can be seen as well as heard. This vision challenges both extremes that often distort Christian witness. On the one hand, it resists withdrawal, where faith is kept private and silent. On the other hand, it resists aggression, where faith is pressed without wisdom or care. Paul charts a different course: thoughtful engagement rooted in Christ.

The emphasis on wisdom also recognises the complexity of the world. Not every question has a simple answer. Not every conversation leads immediately to belief. Faithfulness does not guarantee visible results. What is required is consistency, integrity, and trust in God's work.

Living prayerfully among outsiders

When read alongside Paul's earlier call to devoted prayer, this passage forms a coherent whole. Prayer sustains wisdom. Wisdom guides conduct. Conduct and speech together shape witness. The Church that prays but does not engage becomes inward-looking.

The Church that engages without prayer becomes self-reliant. Paul refuses both options. He calls for a praying people who live wisely and speak graciously. This balance is deeply pastoral. It protects believers from burnout and fear. Witness is not carried by sheer effort. It is shared with God. At the same time, it protects against complacency. Prayer does not excuse inaction.

Paul will soon illustrate these principles through the lives of real people, showing how the gospel moves through relationships, partnerships, and faithful service. But before he does, he establishes the posture the Church must maintain: devoted to prayer, attentive to opportunity, wise in conduct, gracious in speech.

This is not a strategy for success. It is a call to faithfulness. It trusts that God works through ordinary lives lived attentively under Christ's lordship. When believers live this way, the gospel is not merely announced. It is embodied.

Paul now draws together prayer, conduct, and speech into a single, integrated vision of Christian witness. What he has described is not a technique for influence or a strategy for success. It is a way of life shaped by attentiveness to God and attentiveness to people. The Church that lives this way does not need to manufacture relevance. Its life, ordered by Christ, becomes its testimony.

The starting point remains prayer. Devotion to prayer keeps the Church oriented toward God rather than absorbed by its own activity. Watchfulness keeps it alert rather than complacent. Thankfulness keeps it grounded in grace rather than driven by anxiety. These qualities shape the inner posture of believers long before they shape outward behaviour. Prayer, then, is not merely preparation for witness. It is the context in which witness becomes faithful. A praying Church learns to wait, to listen, and to discern. It becomes sensitive to timing and tone. It recognises that God is already at work beyond its own efforts.

A life that invites questions

Paul's call to live wisely toward outsiders assumes that the Christian life will be noticed. Wisdom does not draw attention to itself through display. It becomes visible through consistency, integrity, and restraint. When believers live differently without being defensive or withdrawn, questions naturally arise. This is why Paul emphasises conduct before speech. Our behaviour establishes credibility. It demonstrates whether the message proclaimed has genuinely taken root. A life shaped by grace lends weight to words about grace.

Wisdom toward outsiders also involves humility. Believers are not positioned as judges standing over the world. They live among others as those who themselves depend on mercy. This posture disarms hostility and opens space for honest conversation. Making the most of every opportunity does not mean treating every interaction as a debate. It means recognising moments where listening, kindness, or clarity may serve God's purposes. Wisdom includes knowing when to speak and when to remain silent.

Speech that serves the gospel

When Paul turns to conversation, he places a high value on tone as well as content. Speech full of grace reflects the gospel itself. The message of Christ is not merely true; it is good news. Speech that lacks grace misrepresents the very message it seeks to communicate. Grace-shaped speech resists sarcasm, contempt, and defensiveness. It refuses to reduce people to their objections or disagreements. It remains patient, even when misunderstood. This does not weaken truth. It honours it.

Speech seasoned with salt always adds another dimension. Salt preserves and enhances. In conversation, it brings clarity and interest. Salted speech avoids vagueness and avoids cruelty. It speaks plainly without being harsh and thoughtfully without being evasive. This kind of speech requires attentiveness. Words are chosen with care. Responses are shaped by understanding the person being addressed, not merely by the topic under discussion. Paul's concern is not rhetorical brilliance, but appropriateness.

Knowing how to answer each person

Paul's final phrase (Colossians 4:6) really sharpens the point. Believers are to know "how to answer everyone." The emphasis here is on discernment rather than formula. Different people ask different questions for different reasons. Wise witness listens before it speaks.

Some questions arise from curiosity. Others from pain. Others from scepticism or resistance. A single rehearsed answer cannot serve every situation. Wisdom involves recognising what is actually being asked. This also implies growth. Believers are to deepen their understanding of the gospel so that they can speak with clarity and confidence. At the same time, they are to grow in empathy, so that truth is offered in ways that can be heard. Paul does not place this responsibility on individual brilliance. He places it within a praying community. Prayer keeps believers dependent. Dependence keeps witness humble. Humility keeps speech gracious.

Witness as faithful presence

What emerges from this passage is a vision of witness that is steady rather than sensational. Paul does not promise dramatic results. He calls for faithfulness. Witness is not measured by immediate response, but by consistency under Christ's lordship. The Church bears witness simply by being what it is called to be. A praying people. A watchful people. A thankful people. A wise people. A gracious-speaking people.

This kind of witness resists two common distortions. It resists retreat, where fear leads to silence. And it resists aggression, where urgency overrides wisdom. Paul charts a path that is both courageous and careful. Faithfulness, in this sense, is deeply relational. Witness happens over time, through repeated interactions, shared experiences, and visible character. The gospel is not merely announced. It is embodied in ordinary life.

Living between dependence and responsibility

Paul's instruction holds together two truths that must not be separated. God opens doors. Believers walk through them. God grants clarity. Believers speak faithfully. God works in hearts. Believers live wisely. Prayer does not eliminate responsibility. Responsibility does not replace prayer. Together, they shape a life that honours Christ and serves others.

This balance protects believers from discouragement. Results do not rest entirely on them. It also protects them from passivity. Faithfulness requires attentiveness and effort. Paul's own example stands behind these words. Even in chains, he prays for open doors and clear speech. His circumstances do not dictate his faithfulness. His allegiance to Christ does.

A Church shaped for the world

The calling of the Church comes into focus here. It is not called to dominate the world or to withdraw from it. It is called to live within it as a community shaped by Christ. Prayer keeps the Church rooted. Wisdom guides its conduct. Grace shapes its speech. Discernment directs its responses.

Together, these form a credible and compelling witness. Paul does not promise ease. He promises purpose. Life lived this way becomes a signpost to Christ. Not through force, but through faithfulness. Not through cleverness, but through character.

The invitation is therefore clear. Devote yourselves to prayer. Stay awake to God's work. Give thanks. Live wisely. Speak graciously. Trust God to open doors. And when those doors open, be ready to answer in ways that reflect the grace you yourselves have received. This is the shape of a Church that lives outwardly without losing its centre. It is the shape of a people whose life together points beyond itself to Christ.

How then shall we live?

Colossians 3:18–4:1 brings discipleship into some of the most ordinary and demanding spaces of life: marriage, family, and work. Paul shows that following Christ is not confined to Church gatherings or private spirituality. It is worked out in kitchens and living rooms, in conversations between parents and children, and in workplaces shaped by authority, responsibility, and power. For disciples of Christ today, this passage challenges us to see everyday relationships as arenas of obedience shaped by the lordship of Christ.

First, Paul calls us to live with **Christ at the centre of our closest relationships**. Instructions to wives and husbands are not grounded in cultural convention, they are grounded in belonging "in the Lord" (Colossians 3:18). Marriage, in Paul's vision, is not a contest for control but a shared submission to Christ. For modern disciples, this reframes marriage away from self-fulfilment as the ultimate goal. Love, respect, and mutual responsibility are expressions of obedience to Christ, not merely emotional preference. To live faithfully today means asking not, *What do I want from this relationship?* but, *How does my conduct reflect Christ's lordship here?*

Second, Paul challenges husbands to live with **sacrificial love rather than relational dominance**. "Husbands, love your wives and do not be harsh with them." (Colossians 3:19).

Authority, where it exists, is never permission for cruelty, neglect, or emotional withdrawal. Love here is active, protective, and costly. For disciples today, this confronts any form of relational behaviour that wounds rather than nurtures. Christlike love seeks the good of the other, even at personal cost.

Third, Paul calls families to live with **obedience shaped by care and wisdom**. (Colossians 3:20–21). Children are instructed to obey, while fathers are warned not to embitter or discourage their children. This balance is crucial. Authority without compassion produces resentment, not faithfulness. For disciples today, parenting becomes a form of discipleship itself. Children are not merely to be controlled, but shepherded. Discipline aims at formation, not domination. Encouragement strengthens faith far more effectively than intimidation.

Fourth, Paul extends discipleship decisively into the realm of **work and authority**. Slaves are instructed to obey earthly masters sincerely, not merely when watched, but "with sincerity of heart and reverence for the Lord." (Colossians 3:22). While the social structures differ today, the principle remains deeply relevant. Work is not spiritually neutral. Discipleship shapes how believers approach responsibility, integrity, and effort. To live faithfully today means working not merely for human approval, but as those who serve Christ himself.

Fifth, Paul boldly reframes work by grounding it in **eternal significance**. (Colossians 3:23). "Whatever you do, work at it with all your heart, as working for the Lord, not for human masters." This transforms mundane tasks into acts of worship. Disciples today often struggle with frustration or boredom in work. Paul reminds us that Christ sees faithfulness even when others do not. Our labour is not wasted when it is offered to him.

Sixth, Paul introduces a strong word about **accountability and justice**. God shows no favouritism (Colossians 3:25). This applies to both those under authority and those who exercise it. Disciples today must resist the temptation to justify unfair treatment, exploitation, or abuse of power. Christian obedience never excuses injustice. Instead, it exposes it.

Paul's instruction to masters makes this explicit. "Provide your slaves with what is right and fair, because you know that you also have a Master in heaven." (Colossians 4:1). Authority is relativised by accountability to Christ. For modern disciples in leadership, management, or influence, this is searching. Power is to be exercised with fairness, restraint, and awareness that all authority is temporary and answerable to Christ.

Finally, this passage calls us to live with **integrated discipleship**, not divided lives. Paul does not separate "spiritual" obedience from everyday conduct. Marriage, parenting, and work all fall under Christ's rule. Discipleship today often falters when faith is confined to certain spaces while other areas remain untouched. Paul insists that Christ's lordship reaches into all of life.

So how then shall we live? We live with Christ shaping our closest relationships. We practise love that protects rather than harms. We parent with encouragement as well as authority. We work with integrity and wholeheartedness. We resist injustice and abuse of power. And we remember that in every role we occupy, we serve under the gaze of Christ.

This vision dignifies ordinary life. It assures disciples today that faithfulness in unseen places matters deeply. Where Christ rules our homes and our work, the gospel becomes visible, and everyday obedience becomes an act of worship.

As Paul moves toward the close of his letter, there is a noticeable shift in tone. The great theological declarations have been made. The ethical implications have been pressed home. Prayer, wisdom, and witness have been addressed. Now Paul turns his attention to people – real individuals whose lives and service embody everything he has written so far. What follows is not an appendix to be skimmed, but a vital demonstration of how the gospel works itself out in lived relationships.

Colossians 4:7-9 reminds us that the Christian faith is never merely a set of truths to be believed. It is a life to be shared. The message of Christ advances through faithful people who carry it, explain it, and live it out together.

Paul begins with a trusted companion. "Tychicus will tell you all the news about me." (Colossians 4:7). That simple sentence immediately reveals something important. Paul does not attempt to control every detail or manage every relationship personally. He is willing to entrust his story, his circumstances, and his pastoral care to another believer. The gospel creates a community in which responsibility is shared rather than hoarded.

A faithful messenger in the Lord

Paul does not leave Tychicus undefined. He describes him carefully and deliberately. Tychicus is "a dear brother, a faithful minister and fellow servant in the Lord." (Colossians 4:7). Each phrase adds depth to the picture and reveals how Paul understands Christian ministry.

First, Tychicus is a dear brother. This language speaks of affection and belonging before function. Ministry in the New Testament is never merely transactional. Those who serve together in Christ are bound together as family. Paul does not describe Tychicus primarily by what he does, but by who he is in relationship.

Second, Tychicus is a faithful minister of the gospel. Faithfulness, not prominence, is the defining virtue. Paul does not praise brilliance, charisma, or innovation. He values reliability. A faithful minister is one who can be trusted to carry responsibility consistently, even when the work is costly or unseen.

Third, Tychicus is a fellow servant in the Lord. Paul places himself alongside Tychicus rather than above him. Despite Paul's apostolic authority, he refuses to adopt a posture of superiority. Both men serve the same Lord. Both answer to Christ. This reflects the central theme of the letter: Christ is supreme, and all believers stand under his lordship. This description quietly challenges modern assumptions about leadership. The gospel advances not primarily through celebrity figures, but through faithful servants who labour steadily under Christ's authority.

Encouragement through shared life

Paul then explains why he is sending Tychicus. "I am sending him to you for the express purpose that you may know about our circumstances and that he may encourage your hearts." (Colossians 4:8). Information and encouragement are closely linked. Paul understands that the Colossians need more than facts. They need reassurance, clarity, and strength.

Written words, though inspired and authoritative, are not always enough. The presence of a trusted servant allows for nuance, empathy, and shared experience. Tychicus will not only report on Paul's imprisonment. He will interpret it. He will speak of how God is at work even in confinement. He will strengthen hearts that may be anxious or discouraged.

The word translated "encourage" carries the sense of strengthening or comforting. Paul is deeply pastoral here. He is concerned not only with doctrinal accuracy, but with the emotional and spiritual wellbeing of the Church. A Church under pressure needs encouragement as much as instruction. This also reveals Paul's confidence in God's work through others.

He does not insist on being physically present to care for the Church. He trusts that God will use Tychicus as an instrument of grace. Leadership, in Paul's vision, multiplies rather than centralises.

Onesimus and the power of gospel transformation

Paul now introduces a second companion. "He is coming with Onesimus, our faithful and dear brother, who is one of you." (Colossians 4:9). This sentence is brief, but it carries enormous theological and pastoral weight. Onesimus was not simply another traveller. He was a man with a past. Known elsewhere as a runaway slave, Onesimus had once been defined by failure, shame, and broken relationships. Yet Paul now describes him using the same language he used for Tychicus: faithful and dear brother.

This is the gospel in action. Onesimus is no longer identified by his past sin or social status. He is identified by his new identity in Christ. The grace Paul has proclaimed throughout Colossians is now embodied in a transformed life. By stating that Onesimus is "one of you," Paul reinforces this point even further. Onesimus belongs. He is not returning as a problem to be managed or a failure to be tolerated. He returns as a brother to be received. The Church is called to see him not through the lens of history, but through the lens of grace.

This is not sentimental language. It is costly obedience. To receive Onesimus as a brother may require forgiveness, humility, and the dismantling of social assumptions. Paul is quietly calling the Church to live out the reconciling power of the gospel in tangible ways.

The Gospel Moves Through Relationships

Paul concludes this section with a simple summary. "They will tell you everything that is happening here." (Colossians 4:9). Once again, the emphasis is on shared life and shared knowledge. The gospel does not advance through isolation. It advances through connection.

Paul's imprisonment has not halted the mission. Instead, it has created new pathways for encouragement, testimony, and growth. Tychicus and Onesimus become living links between Paul and the Colossian Church. Through them both, faith is strengthened and unity is preserved.

This passage reminds us that much of Christian ministry is ordinary and relational. It involves trusted messengers, honest communication, and gentle, patient encouragement. God works powerfully through these means, even though they may appear unimpressive by worldly standards.

Lessons for the Church today

Colossians 4:7-9 challenges the Church to rethink how it understands effectiveness and success. The advance of the gospel does not depend solely on gifted leaders or dramatic events. It depends on faithful people who are willing to serve, travel, speak, and encourage. The Church needs people like Tychicus - reliable, humble, and committed to strengthening others. It needs people like Onesimus - living testimonies to grace, whose transformed lives point to the power of Christ. It needs communities willing to receive such people with open hearts.

This passage also reminds believers that the gospel is deeply personal. Theology is not detached from relationships. Christ's supremacy is displayed not only in doctrine, but in the way believers treat one another. As Paul's letter nears its end, he shows that the truth of Christ produces a people marked by faithfulness, encouragement, and reconciliation. The message that began with the supremacy of Christ now takes flesh in the lives of those who serve Him together.

The gospel does not merely inform the mind. It reshapes identity, restores relationships, and binds believers together in shared service. In Tychicus and Onesimus, we see that truth lived out. Paul's brief comments about Tychicus and Onesimus continue to unfold a deeply pastoral vision of how the gospel moves through ordinary faithfulness.

What we see here is not simply the transmission of information, but the shaping of a community that understands itself as bound together in Christ. The gospel does not travel as an abstract message detached from people. It travels through lives marked by trust, service, and reconciliation.

The decision to send Tychicus is itself quite revealing. Paul is imprisoned, limited in movement and communication, yet he refuses to allow those limitations to isolate him from the Churches. He does not retreat inward. Instead, he sends a trusted servant to maintain connection.

This reflects a conviction that the Church must remain relationally connected, even when circumstances make that difficult. Tychicus is entrusted with more than facts. He carries Paul's heart. He will speak about Paul's chains, but he will also speak about Paul's hope, courage, and confidence in Christ. The Colossians will not merely hear what has happened. They will hear how Paul is enduring, and how the gospel continues to bear fruit even in confinement.

Faithfulness as a mark of gospel service

Paul's description of Tychicus as faithful invites reflection on what faithfulness really means. Faithfulness is not spectacular. It does not draw attention to itself. It is steady, dependable obedience over time. In a culture that prizes visibility and achievement, Paul highlights something quieter and more enduring.

Tychicus is faithful because he can be trusted with responsibility. He can be trusted to speak accurately, to care pastorally, and to represent Paul truthfully. Faithfulness here includes integrity, discretion, and consistency. These are qualities essential to gospel ministry, yet often overlooked. Paul's emphasis reminds the Church that the advance of the gospel depends on people who are willing to serve without recognition. Faithful servants are often invisible, but they are indispensable. Without them, connection frays, encouragement weakens, and ministry becomes fragile. This then challenges how believers measure usefulness.

Faithfulness is not measured by prominence, but by reliability. It is shaped by allegiance to Christ rather than by human approval. Tychicus serves not because his role is impressive, but because Christ is Lord.

Encouragement that strengthens the heart

Paul's concern for encouragement deserves careful attention. He does not assume that the Colossians will automatically interpret his imprisonment correctly. He knows that suffering can unsettle faith. Questions may arise. Doubts may creep in. Encouragement becomes a necessary ministry. The strengthening of hearts is a recurring pastoral concern in Paul's letters. Hearts can grow weary, fearful, or discouraged under pressure. Encouragement is not mere cheerfulness. It is the ministry of helping believers interpret their circumstances in light of Christ's lordship.

Tychicus will encourage by reminding the Colossians that Paul's chains do not signal defeat. They are part of faithful witness. God's purposes are not thwarted by confinement. The gospel is not fragile. It advances even through suffering.

This encouragement works both ways. The Colossians, strengthened by Tychicus's report, will in turn be encouraged to remain steadfast. Their faithfulness supports Paul just as his faithfulness supports them. The Church is sustained through mutual encouragement grounded in Christ.

Onesimus and the new identity in Christ

The presence of Onesimus alongside Tychicus deepens this picture significantly. Onesimus embodies the transforming power of the gospel in a personal and visible way. His story illustrates that the gospel does not merely declare forgiveness. It creates new identity. By calling Onesimus faithful and dear, Paul signals that Onesimus has proven trustworthy. Faithfulness here implies change over time. Onesimus's past no longer defines his present. His new life in Christ has reshaped his character and commitments. This transformation is not merely internal. It has relational consequences.

Onesimus is returning to Colossae not as a fugitive, but as a brother. The gospel now governs how he is to be received. Social categories that once defined him are relativised by his belonging in Christ. Paul's phrasing, "who is one of you." (Colossians 4:9), presses this point home. Onesimus belongs fully to the community. He is not marginal. He is not provisional. He is one of them. The Church is called to recognise what Christ has done and to align its relationships accordingly. This challenges any tendency to keep people permanently defined by their past. The gospel insists that new creation is real. To deny restored belonging is to deny the power of grace. Paul's language gently but firmly directs the Church toward obedience shaped by reconciliation.

The cost of receiving one another

Receiving Onesimus as a brother may not be easy. It may involve confronting unresolved tension, social awkwardness, or personal hurt. Paul does not minimise these realities. Instead, he places them within the larger framework of Christ's lordship.

Throughout Colossians, Paul has insisted that Christ is supreme over every power and authority. That supremacy must now be expressed in how believers treat one another. Social hierarchies, grievances, and fears must yield to the reconciling work of Christ. The presence of Onesimus alongside Tychicus is therefore intentional. It demonstrates that gospel ministry includes restored relationships, not just right teaching. The message Paul proclaims about reconciliation is being lived out in real time. This reminds the Church that obedience often involves discomfort. Grace is costly because it requires relinquishing control and embracing Christ's priorities. Yet it is precisely in these moments that the gospel becomes visible.

The gospel shared through trust

Paul's closing statement in this section underscores the simplicity and depth of what is taking place. "They will tell you everything that is happening here." (Colossians 4:9). There is transparency rather than secrecy. Trust rather than control.

Paul entrusts his story to others. He allows the Church to see his weakness as well as his faith. This openness strengthens community. It reminds believers that the gospel is lived out in real circumstances, not idealised conditions.

This shared knowledge binds the Church together. The Colossians are not spectators of Paul's ministry. They are participants through prayer, concern, and shared identity. The gospel advances not only through preaching, but through the bonds of mutual trust.

A pattern for gospel-shaped community

Colossians 4:7–9 offers a pattern for the Church in every age. The gospel moves through faithful servants who can be trusted. It strengthens hearts through honest encouragement. It restores lives and relationships through grace. It binds communities together through shared life.

This passage resists individualism. Ministry is never a solo endeavour. Even an apostle depends on others. The Church thrives when believers recognise their interdependence and serve one another under Christ's lordship.

Paul's vision is clear. The supremacy of Christ produces a people marked by faithfulness, encouragement, and reconciliation. The gospel is not only proclaimed. It is carried, embodied, and lived out through ordinary believers who serve together in the Lord.

In Tychicus and Onesimus, the Colossians are invited to see what the gospel looks like when it takes root in human lives. The message they have received is now coming to them in flesh and blood. And through that living witness, their faith is strengthened, their community is shaped, and Christ is honoured.

As Paul concludes this brief but rich section, the emphasis remains on how the gospel is carried forward through trustworthy people and transformed relationships. Paul does not introduce new doctrine. He simply shows doctrine in motion.

The supremacy of Christ, the reconciliation accomplished through the cross, and the new identity of believers are all assumed realities. What Paul now highlights is how those realities are expressed through everyday faithfulness.

The Christian life, as Paul presents it, is never detached from people. It is lived out through relationships marked by trust, humility, and grace. The sending of Tychicus and Onesimus is not a logistical detail to be skimmed. It is a pastoral strategy shaped by the gospel itself.

Shared ministry under Christ's Lordship

One of the most striking features of this passage is Paul's refusal to act alone. Though he is an apostle with unique authority, he does not insist on personal control. He shares responsibility willingly. Tychicus is entrusted to speak on Paul's behalf. Onesimus is entrusted with a message that his own life embodies. This shared ministry reflects Paul's understanding of Christ's lordship. Because Christ is supreme, no servant needs to assert supremacy. Authority is exercised through service rather than dominance. Paul's leadership is confident enough to be generous. He empowers others because he trusts the Lord they all serve.

This challenges any model of ministry built on control or personality. The gospel advances not when everything flows through one individual, but when responsibility is shared among faithful servants. Paul's confidence is not in structures or strategies, but in Christ working through his people. The Church is strongest when it recognises this shared calling. No believer carries the gospel alone. Each part of the body contributes, and each contribution matters. Tychicus's reliability and Onesimus's transformed life are equally essential to the mission.

Truth communicated through trust

Paul's willingness to entrust his circumstances to others also reveals something about how truth is meant to be communicated. The gospel does not travel through manipulation or spin. It travels through honesty and trust.

By sending Tychicus to explain his situation, Paul allows the Colossians to hear not only what is happening, but how it is being interpreted through faith. Tychicus will speak of chains, but he will also speak of hope. He will speak of hardship, but also of God's faithfulness. This kind of communication strengthens the Church. It prevents speculation and fear. It anchors faith in reality, rather than rumour.

Paul understands that a well-informed Church is a resilient Church. This principle still matters. Christian community is sustained when believers speak truthfully about both joy and struggle. Faith does not require denial. It requires trust in Christ amid reality. Paul models a leadership that is transparent without being despairing, honest without being self-pitying.

The gospel's demand for reconciled relationships

The inclusion of Onesimus adds another layer of depth to this passage. Onesimus is not merely accompanying Tychicus. He is a living demonstration of the gospel's reconciling power. Paul's description of Onesimus as faithful and dear underscores that transformation is not theoretical.

Onesimus has proven trustworthy. His life has changed. Grace has taken root and borne fruit. This transformation, however, now places a responsibility on the Church. To receive Onesimus as a brother requires obedience. The Colossians must align their relationships with the reality of the gospel they profess. Grace received must become grace extended.

This is where the cost of discipleship becomes really clear. Reconciliation often requires humility, forgiveness, and a willingness to relinquish old categories. The gospel does not merely challenge personal sin. It challenges social assumptions and relational patterns.

Paul does not spell this out explicitly, but the implication is unmistakable. If Christ has reconciled Onesimus to God, the Church must not refuse to reconcile with him. Anything less would deny the very message they claim to believe.

Belonging as a mark of new creation

Paul's phrase "who is one of you." (Colossians 4:9) deserves careful attention. Belonging is not treated as conditional or provisional. Onesimus belongs because he belongs to Christ. This belonging redefines identity.

In Christ, believers are no longer primarily identified by ethnicity, status, or past failure. They are identified by grace. Paul has already made this clear earlier in the letter. Now he shows what it looks like in practice.

The Church is called to be a community where new creation is recognised and honoured. This does not mean ignoring the past. It means refusing to allow the past to determine the future. Onesimus's story becomes part of the Church's story.

This has enduring relevance. Churches must continually ask whether their life together reflects the reconciling power of the gospel. Are people welcomed as Christ has welcomed them. Are restored lives truly embraced. Is belonging grounded in grace rather than conformity.

Encouragement through embodied witness

The arrival of Tychicus and Onesimus will encourage the Colossians not only through words, but through presence. They will see faithfulness embodied. They will hear testimony firsthand. They will be reminded that the gospel is alive and active beyond their immediate context.

Paul understands the power of embodied witness. Letters will instruct. People will inspire. The presence of faithful servants strengthens faith in ways written words alone cannot.

is why Paul places such value on sending people, not just messages. This also highlights the relational nature of encouragement. Encouragement is not abstract. It happens through shared stories, shared struggles, and shared hope. Tychicus and Onesimus will bring with them the reality of Paul's perseverance and the evidence of God's work.

The Gospel advancing through ordinary faithfulness

The significance of Colossians 4:7–9 now becomes very clear. The gospel advances not only through proclamation, but through faithful service, honest communication, and reconciled relationships.

Paul's chains have not silenced the gospel. They have simply shifted how it moves. Faithful servants step forward. Encouragement is multiplied. Grace is displayed through restored lives. This passage invites the Church to value what God values. Faithfulness over fame. Reliability over recognition. Reconciliation over resentment. Community over isolation.

The supremacy of Christ, proclaimed so powerfully earlier in the letter, now finds expression in the lives of ordinary believers who serve together under his lordship. Tychicus and Onesimus are not heroes in the conventional sense. They are servants. And in that, they reflect the heart of the gospel.

The call to the Church is therefore clear. Trust one another. Encourage one another. Receive one another as Christ has received you. Allow the gospel to shape not only what you believe, but how you live together. When the gospel takes root in this way, it becomes visible. Christ is honoured. The Church is strengthened. And the good news continues to move, carried by faithful people, from one heart to another.

How then shall we live?

Colossians 4:7–9 brings discipleship down to ground level. After all the rich theology and searching exhortation of the letter, Paul draws our attention to ordinary people, faithful service, and transformed relationships. Tychicus and Onesimus are not presented as heroes of dramatic achievement, but as living demonstrations of what the gospel produces.

For disciples of Christ today, this passage challenges how we understand faithfulness, community, and the everyday ways God advances his work.

First, this passage calls us to live with a **deep respect for ordinary faithfulness**. (Colossians 4:7). Tychicus is described as a dear brother, a faithful minister, and a fellow servant in the Lord. None of these titles suggest prominence or public recognition. They speak of reliability, humility, and consistency. Discipleship today is often shaped by visible success – influence, growth, or platform. Paul points us instead toward trustworthiness. To live faithfully now is to recognise that much of God's work is carried forward by people who show up, follow through, and serve quietly. Faithfulness over time matters more than visibility in the moment.

Second, Paul invites us to live as people who **strengthen one another through encouragement and honest communication**. Tychicus is sent not only to inform the Church about Paul's circumstances, but to encourage their hearts (Colossians 4:8). Encouragement here is not shallow positivity. It is truth shared in love. Disciples today live faithfully when they resist isolation and choose instead to speak honestly about both hardship and hope. Churches grow resilient when believers learn to encourage one another with realistic faith rather than spiritual pretence.

Third, this passage calls us to live with a **shared understanding of ministry rather than individual ownership**. Paul does not insist on being the sole voice or authority. He entrusts his message and pastoral care to others. Discipleship today often struggles with control – either the desire to dominate or the fear of responsibility. Paul models a different way. To live faithfully is to recognise that the work of Christ belongs to the whole body. Ministry is multiplied when responsibility is shared and trust is extended.

Fourth, the presence of Onesimus calls us to live with a **gospel-shaped view of identity**. Onesimus is no longer introduced by his past failure or social status. He is described as a faithful and dear brother, one who belongs (Colossians 4:9). This is a powerful reminder for disciples today. The gospel does not merely forgive the past; it redefines the present. To live faithfully is to refuse to define ourselves or others primarily by past sin, mistakes, or labels.

In Christ, new identity is real. Churches must learn to see people as God sees them – not as they were, but as those being renewed in Christ.

Fifth, this passage challenges us to live with **courageous commitment to reconciliation**. Onesimus's return to Colossae is not comfortable or convenient. It requires humility, forgiveness, and obedience from everyone involved. Discipleship today often avoids relational difficulty by keeping distance or harbouring quiet resentment. Paul shows us that the gospel moves toward reconciliation, not away from it. To live faithfully now is to allow grace to shape how we repair broken relationships, even when it is costly.

Sixth, Paul's words invite us to live with a **realistic view of Christian community**. The gospel advances through people who carry news, speak truth, and embody grace. This is slow, relational work. Disciples today are sometimes tempted to believe that impact requires constant innovation or dramatic change. Paul reminds us that God often works through patient, relational faithfulness. Letters are carried. Stories are told. Hearts are encouraged. The Church is strengthened quietly but genuinely.

Seventh, this passage calls us to live with **humility about our role in God's work**. Paul's imprisonment has not halted the gospel. It has simply changed how it moves. Disciples today may become discouraged when plans are disrupted or circumstances limit what we can do. Paul shows that God's purposes are not fragile. When one door closes, others open. Faithfulness does not depend on ideal conditions. To live faithfully is to trust that God remains at work even when our own role feels reduced or altered.

Eighth, this passage urges us to live as people who **value presence as much as proclamation**. Tychicus and Onesimus do not merely deliver information. They embody the message. Their presence strengthens faith. Discipleship today often overvalues content while undervaluing presence.

Yet much spiritual encouragement comes not from perfect words, but from faithful companionship. To live well is to be present with others in ways that reflect Christ's care.

Finally, this text calls us to live with **confidence that God works through faithful people, not perfect ones**. Tychicus is faithful. Onesimus is transformed. Neither is presented as flawless. God uses them as they are, shaped by grace.

Disciples today often hesitate to serve because they feel inadequate or unqualified. Paul's example reassures us that God delights to work through those who are willing, dependable, and shaped by the gospel.

So how then shall we live? We live by valuing faithfulness over recognition. We encourage one another with truth and hope. We share responsibility rather than clinging to control. We see ourselves and others through the lens of new identity in Christ. We pursue reconciliation rather than avoidance. We trust God's work in changing circumstances. We practise presence as a form of ministry. And we step forward in service, confident that grace equips us for faithful obedience.

This is discipleship at ground level – ordinary lives shaped by an extraordinary gospel, carrying Christ's work forward through faithfulness, humility, and grace.

9. FAITHFUL SERVANTS, REAL RELATIONSHIPS
(Colossians 4:10-14)

As Paul continues his closing greetings, the letter takes on an even more personal texture. Names are listed, relationships are referenced, and brief comments are offered about those who stand alongside him in ministry. Yet this is far more than a list of acknowledgements. In Colossians 4:10–14, Paul shows us what gospel partnership looks like in real life. The advance of the gospel is never the work of one person alone. It is sustained through faithful servants, restored relationships, persevering prayer, and shared encouragement.

Paul's theology has been rich and demanding. Christ is supreme. Believers are united with him. Old ways of life are put to death, and new life is embraced. Prayer, wisdom, and gracious witness are essential. Now Paul shows how all of this is embodied in a network of people whose lives have been shaped by Christ.

Faithfulness shared in suffering

Paul begins by mentioning Aristarchus. "My fellow prisoner Aristarchus sends you his greetings." (Colossians 4:10). With this simple description, Paul highlights solidarity in suffering. Aristarchus is not merely a visitor or a casual associate. He shares Paul's imprisonment. He has chosen to remain close despite the cost.

Suffering for the sake of the gospel is not romanticised here. Paul does not dwell on hardship, but neither does he hide it. The presence of a fellow prisoner reminds the Church that faithfulness can involve real loss and limitation. At the same time, it shows that suffering does not isolate believers from one another.

True community endures even in confinement. Aristarchus's faithfulness offers quiet encouragement. He stands as evidence that perseverance is possible. Faithful companionship in hardship strengthens resolve and guards against despair. Paul honours this by naming him and acknowledging his presence.

Restoration and welcome in the work of God

Paul next refers to Mark, the cousin of Barnabas. "You have received instructions about him; if he comes to you, welcome him." (Colossians 4:10). This brief instruction carries a significant backstory. Earlier in Paul's ministry, Mark had withdrawn from a missionary journey, leading to sharp disagreement between Paul and Barnabas. That failure could have easily ended Mark's usefulness permanently. Instead, here he stands restored and commended. Paul's words signal reconciliation and renewed trust.

The instruction to welcome Mark is deliberate. It prepares the Church to receive him not with suspicion, but with openness. The gospel makes room for restoration. Failure is not the final word. Grace can renew both calling and confidence. This moment quietly reinforces one of the letter's central themes. New creation in Christ is real. It reshapes not only personal identity, but communal relationships. To welcome Mark is to align the Church's practice with the grace it proclaims. Paul then mentions Jesus, who is called Justus. "These are the only Jews among my co-workers for the kingdom of God, and they have proved a comfort to me." (Colossians 4:11).

This statement is both encouraging and sobering. Paul acknowledges that only a few from his Jewish background are labouring alongside him. Many have rejected his message and his ministry. Yet those who remain are deeply valued. Their presence has been a comfort to him.

This comfort is not trivial. Ministry can be lonely, especially when opposition comes from expected allies. Faithful companions sustain courage. Paul's words remind the Church that encouragement often comes through people who simply remain present and loyal.

Epaphras and the hidden labour of prayer

Paul now turns to Epaphras, a figure closely connected to the Colossians. "Epaphras, who is one of you and a servant of Christ Jesus, sends greetings." (Colossians 4:12).

By identifying Epaphras as "one of you," Paul strengthens the bond between him and the Church. Epaphras is described as a servant of Christ Jesus, and Paul highlights the distinctive shape of his ministry. Epaphras is "always wrestling in prayer for you." (Colossians 4:12). The language is vivid and demanding. Prayer is presented not as a gentle pastime, but as strenuous effort. The word translated "wrestling" suggests struggle, persistence, and intensity. Epaphras' ministry may be largely unseen, but it is not passive. He labours on behalf of the Church through sustained intercession.

Paul also reveals the content of Epaphras' prayers. He longs for the Colossians to "stand firm in all the will of God, mature and fully assured." (Colossians 4:12). These are deeply pastoral concerns. Epaphras is not primarily focused on numbers, reputation, or novelty. He desires stability, maturity, and assurance grounded in God's will. This reminds the Church that prayer is one of the most significant forms of ministry. Growth in Christ often depends on unseen faithfulness rather than visible activity. Epaphras' prayers support the Church at its deepest points of need.

Paul affirms this labour openly. "I vouch for him that he is working hard for you and for those at Laodicea and Hierapolis." (Colossians 4:13). Prayer is real work. It is demanding, costly, and essential. Paul ensures that Epaphras' hidden labour is publicly recognised.

Gifts and realities within gospel partnership

Paul now mentions Luke and Demas. "Our dear friend Luke, the doctor, and Demas send greetings." (Colossians 4:14). With these names, Paul subtly reminds the Church that gospel partnership includes people with different gifts and trajectories. Luke is described as a dear friend, and his profession is noted. His medical skill likely served the missionary team in practical ways. The gospel does not erase vocation. It redeems it. Luke's faithfulness includes both spiritual commitment and practical service. Demas is mentioned without description.

At this point, he stands among Paul's companions. There is no hint of what lies ahead. Paul's restraint is instructive. Ministry is lived in real time, with real people, some of whom persevere and some of whom later falter.

This realism grounds the Church's expectations. Faithfulness is not automatic. It is sustained through grace, encouragement, and dependence on Christ. Paul neither idealises nor despairs. He simply acknowledges those currently labouring alongside him.

The shape of gospel community

Taken together, these verses paint a rich picture of gospel community. Faithful companions share suffering. Restored servants are welcomed. Prayer sustains growth. Diverse gifts serve a common purpose. Encouragement strengthens perseverance. The advance of the gospel depends on people who are willing to remain faithful in different ways.

Some travel. Some pray. Some offer practical care. Some simply stay. All contribute to the work of God. Paul's greetings remind the Church that Christ's supremacy is not abstract. It is expressed through lives shaped by grace and commitment. The gospel creates a people who belong to one another, serve together, and endure together. Through these real relationships, Paul shows that faithful service and genuine connection are not peripheral to the gospel. They are essential to its ongoing work in the world.

Paul's closing greetings continue to unfold a theology of ministry that is deeply relational and quietly demanding. What becomes increasingly clear is that the gospel does not advance through impersonal systems or solitary heroes, but through people whose lives are bound together by Christ. In these verses, Paul shows the Colossians not only *who* is with him, but *how* gospel partnership actually works in practice. The individuals Paul names are not interchangeable pieces in a ministry machine. Each has a distinct story, role, and contribution. Yet they are united by a shared allegiance to Christ and a shared commitment to the work of the kingdom. Their differences do not weaken the mission. They enrich it.

Comfort in shared labour

Paul's brief statement that his Jewish co-workers "have proved a comfort to me." (Colossians 4:11) deserves careful reflection. Comfort here does not imply ease or emotional indulgence. It speaks of strengthening, reassurance, and support that enables perseverance. Paul's ministry has involved sustained opposition, misunderstanding, and isolation. Many from his own background have rejected his message. In that context, the presence of a few faithful companions carries enormous weight. Their solidarity affirms that Paul has not laboured in vain and that the gospel has not failed.

This reminder speaks powerfully to the nature of Christian encouragement. Encouragement is not always dramatic or verbal. Often it comes through presence, loyalty, and shared burden. To stand alongside someone in difficulty is itself a ministry. The Church must not underestimate this kind of faithfulness. Many believers will never preach publicly or travel widely. Yet by remaining present, supportive, and prayerful, they become a source of real strength to others. Paul's words honour this quieter contribution.

The cost and reward of gospel partnership

Partnership in the gospel is not without cost. Aristarchus's imprisonment, Mark's earlier failure, and Paul's ongoing confinement all remind us that ministry is demanding. Faithfulness often requires sacrifice, patience, and resilience. Yet Paul does not present these costs as reasons for discouragement. He presents them as contexts in which God's grace is displayed. Restoration becomes visible. Loyalty becomes precious. Prayer becomes essential.

Mark's presence alongside Paul is particularly instructive here. The gospel does not demand flawless records. It produces restored servants. Mark's earlier withdrawal did not disqualify him permanently. Grace reopened the door to service. This should shape how the Church understands failure. Failure, though serious, is not necessarily final.

When repentance and growth are evident, restoration honours the gospel more than permanent exclusion. Paul's instruction to welcome Mark reflects confidence in God's transforming work.

Epaphras and the priority of spiritual maturity

Paul's description of Epaphras returns us again to the heart of pastoral concern. Epaphras' prayers focus on one central aim: that the Colossians might stand firm, mature, and fully assured in God's will (Colossians 4:12). This reveals a great deal about what genuine spiritual maturity looks like. It is not defined by novelty, intensity, or constant change. It is defined by stability, depth, and assurance rooted in God's purposes.

To stand firm implies resistance against pressure. The Colossians face false teaching and cultural influence that threaten to destabilise their faith. Epaphras prays not for escape from difficulty, but for strength to remain faithful within it. Maturity involves growth toward completeness. Paul has already emphasised that fullness is found in Christ. Epaphras' prayers align perfectly with that theology. He desires that believers grow deeper in Christ rather than chasing substitutes.

Full assurance speaks of settled confidence. It is the opposite of anxiety-driven spirituality. Epaphras longs for the Colossians to know where they stand with God and to live out of that security. This kind of assurance produces endurance rather than complacency. Paul's public affirmation of Epaphras' labour reinforces the value of this kind of ministry. Prayer that aims at maturity may not produce immediate visible results, but it shapes the long-term health of the Church.

Unseen labour and God's recognition

Paul's statement that Epaphras is "working hard for you." (Colossians 4:13) challenges common assumptions about what counts as real work. Prayer, though unseen, is labour. Intercession requires time, energy, and perseverance. The modern tendency to value what is visible and measurable can lead to neglect of prayer.

Paul corrects this by placing Epaphras' intercession alongside other forms of ministry. Prayer is not an alternative to work. It is work. This recognition should encourage those believers whose service feels hidden. God sees what others may often overlook. Faithful labour, whether public or private, matters in God's economy. Paul's words here ensure that Epaphras' ministry is honoured and remembered. This also places responsibility on the Church. Prayerful labour should be supported, valued, and shared. A Church that neglects prayer undermines its own strength. A Church that honours prayer invests in its future faithfulness.

Diversity of gifts within one mission

The mention of Luke and Demas reminds the Church that gospel partnership includes people with diverse gifts and varying trajectories. Luke's medical expertise serves the mission practically, while his companionship supports Paul personally. The inclusion of Demas, without commentary, adds realism.

At this point, Demas is present and involved. Paul does not speculate about the future. He acknowledges current faithfulness while recognising that perseverance cannot be assumed.

This realism guards the Church against both naïve optimism and cynical suspicion. Faithfulness is to be encouraged, not presumed. Relationships require ongoing nurture. The gospel community lives by grace, not by guarantees.

A community sustained by grace

What emerges from these verses is a portrait of a community sustained by grace at every level. Grace restores the fallen. Grace strengthens the weary. Grace sustains prayer. Grace holds diverse people together in shared mission. Paul's greetings are therefore not peripheral to the letter's message. They are its embodiment. The supremacy of Christ creates a people who serve together, forgive one another, pray persistently, and persevere faithfully. This challenges individualistic approaches to faith.

Christianity is not a private spiritual journey which is detached from others. It is a shared life under Christ's lordship. Growth happens in community. Perseverance is supported by others. Faithfulness is sustained together.

As we continue in this passage, Paul will further emphasise responsibility, accountability, and perseverance within the Church. But even here, the lesson is clear. The gospel advances through people who remain faithful in both visible and unseen ways.

The Colossians are invited to see themselves as part of this wider story. They are not isolated believers. They belong to a network of grace-shaped relationships. And within that network, every act of faithfulness, prayer, and encouragement matters.

As Paul's greetings draw this section toward completion, the emphasis sharpens around perseverance, responsibility, and the sustaining grace of God within gospel partnership. The people named in Colossians 4:10–14 are not presented as idealised figures. They are real servants navigating pressure, weakness, endurance, and hope. Through them, Paul shows that faithfulness over time is one of the clearest evidences of the gospel at work.

What binds these individuals together is not shared temperament or identical calling, but shared allegiance to Christ. Their unity is not the result of convenience. It is the fruit of grace shaping diverse lives toward a common purpose.

Perseverance as a gospel reality

Paul's references throughout this passage quietly highlight the necessity of perseverance. Aristarchus remains imprisoned. Mark has returned after earlier failure. Epaphras labours relentlessly in prayer. Luke continues faithfully alongside Paul.

Even Demas, mentioned without elaboration, reminds us that ministry is lived in the present tense, where endurance is required day by day.

Perseverance is not portrayed here as heroic determination. It is sustained obedience rooted in confidence that Christ is Lord. Paul has already made clear earlier in the letter that believers are complete in Christ. That theological foundation now bears practical fruit. Because Christ is sufficient, believers can endure.

This matters deeply for the Church. Faithfulness is often tested not in moments of dramatic decision, but in long seasons of ordinary obedience. Paul honours those who remain, who continue, and who do not abandon their calling when it becomes costly or unspectacular. The presence of restored and persevering servants encourages the Colossians to remain steadfast. The gospel they believe is not fragile. It sustains people over time.

Encouragement without illusion

One of the striking features of Paul's language is its honesty. He does not claim that ministry is easy or uniformly successful. He acknowledges imprisonment, limited support, and ongoing struggle. Yet his tone is neither bitter nor defensive. This balance is instructive. Paul refuses to create illusions about Christian service. Faithfulness does not guarantee comfort. Obedience does not eliminate difficulty. Yet hardship does not signal failure. It often accompanies faithfulness.

Encouragement in this context does not come from denying reality, but from interpreting reality through Christ's lordship. Paul's companions are encouraged not because circumstances are ideal, but because Christ remains supreme. This kind of encouragement strengthens the Church. It prepares believers to face difficulty without surprise or despair. It roots hope not in outcomes, but in the unchanging faithfulness of God.

Prayer as the engine of endurance

Epaphras' ministry continues to stand at the very centre of this passage as a reminder of what sustains perseverance. His wrestling in prayer reveals that endurance is not maintained by willpower alone. It is sustained through dependence on God.

Paul's affirmation of Epaphras' labour reinforces the truth that prayer undergirds every other form of service. Teaching, travel, encouragement, and restoration all depend on prayer. Without it, ministry becomes fragile and reactive.

The content of Epaphras' prayers remains deeply significant. He prays for maturity, firmness, and assurance. These are the very qualities required for perseverance. Believers who are unsure of their standing with God or unstable in their faith are vulnerable to discouragement.

Prayer that aims at maturity strengthens the Church at its core. It builds resilience rather than excitement, depth rather than novelty. Paul's public recognition of this prayerful labour teaches the Church what to value.

Faithfulness over time

Luke's quiet presence alongside Paul underscores the importance of steady faithfulness. Luke is not described with dramatic language. He is simply present, continuing to serve. His medical skill and companionship likely made Paul's imprisonment more bearable, yet Paul does not dwell on details.

This understated recognition reflects a broader biblical pattern. Much of faithful service is ordinary. It does not draw attention. It is expressed through consistency, reliability, and care over time. Such faithfulness often goes unnoticed, yet it is essential. The Church depends on people who continue showing up, continuing serving, and continuing trusting Christ. Luke's presence affirms that such faithfulness matters deeply in God's work.

Demas's inclusion without commentary also reinforces the seriousness of perseverance. At this moment, Demas is part of the team. Paul neither praises nor criticises him. The absence of evaluation reminds the Church that perseverance must be nurtured and guarded. Faithfulness is not automatic. It is sustained through grace, accountability, and dependence on Christ.

A community shaped by grace

When these individuals are considered together, a clear picture of gospel community emerges. Grace restores those who stumble. Grace strengthens those who suffer. Grace sustains those who pray. Grace holds together people of different backgrounds and roles.

This community is not built on shared success, but on shared submission to Christ. Each person serves according to the grace given to them. No role is insignificant. No act of faithfulness is wasted. Paul's greetings therefore function as more than acknowledgements. They teach the Church how to view one another. Faithfulness is to be honoured. Prayer is to be valued. Restoration is to be embraced. Perseverance is to be encouraged.

The gospel lived together

Colossians 4:10–14 shows that the gospel does not merely create individual believers. It creates a people. That people is sustained not by perfection, but by grace at work in real lives. Paul's earlier teaching about Christ's supremacy now finds some concrete expression. Because Jesus Christ is Lord, believers can endure suffering without despair, restore those who fall, labour in prayer without recognition, and remain faithful in ordinary service.

This passage invites the Church to measure success differently. The question is not who appears impressive, but who remains faithful. It is not who receives attention, but who continues to serve under Christ's lordship. The Colossians are encouraged to see themselves as part of this same story. They too are called to perseverance, prayer, restoration, and shared service. The gospel that has reached them continues to advance through faithful people like those Paul names.

The message here is clear. The work of Christ is sustained through ordinary faithfulness shaped by extraordinary grace. Where believers remain rooted in Christ, support one another, and labour together, the gospel continues to bear fruit.

Christ remains supreme. Grace remains sufficient. And faithful service, offered day by day, becomes the means through which God's purposes endure.

How then shall we live?

Colossians 4:15–18 brings the letter to a close, but it does not wind discipleship down. Instead, Paul presses the life of faith into its most enduring shape: perseverance which is rooted in Scripture, responsibility embraced within community, suffering remembered honestly, and grace relied upon continually. For disciples of Christ today, this final passage calls us to a long obedience sustained not by intensity, but by faithfulness under Christ's lordship.

First, this passage calls us to live as people who are **shaped by God's word together, not in isolation**. Paul's instruction that his letter be read publicly and shared with neighbouring Churches (4:16) reminds us that Scripture is fundamentally communal. Discipleship today often becomes individualised, reduced to private reading detached from shared accountability.

Paul envisions something richer. The word of Christ is meant to be heard, wrestled with, and obeyed together. To live faithfully now is to resist a pick-and-choose approach to Scripture and to commit ourselves to being formed by God's word within the gathered people of God. This includes listening humbly, allowing Scripture to challenge cherished assumptions, and submitting our lives to its authority rather than merely using it for inspiration or affirmation.

Second, Paul calls us to live with **responsibility toward the ministries entrusted to us** in his direct word to Archippus – "See to it that you complete the ministry you have received in the Lord." (Colossians 4:17). is not only personal but representative. Every disciple has received some form of calling, responsibility, or trust from Christ. It may not be public or prominent, but it is real. To live faithfully today is to take that calling seriously. Completion matters. Not comparison. Not visibility.

In a culture that celebrates beginnings and novelty, Paul reminds us that faithfulness is measured by perseverance. Discipleship is not proven by how enthusiastically we start, but by how faithfully we continue.

Third, this passage challenges us to always live with **mutual accountability rather than maintain private spirituality**. Paul's exhortation to Archippus is delivered through the Church. This implies that perseverance in ministry is not meant to be solitary. Disciples today often struggle alone, quietly questioning whether their service still matters or whether they should continue. Paul shows us a better way. The Church is called to speak encouragement, offer reminder, and provide support so that believers do not abandon what Christ has entrusted to them. To live faithfully now is to allow others to speak into our calling and to accept encouragement as God's provision rather than personal intrusion.

Fourth, Paul calls us to live with **a sober and honest view of suffering**. His simple appeal, "Remember my chains." (Colossians 4:18), anchors discipleship in reality. Faithfulness to Christ may involve limitation, misunderstanding, or cost. Paul does not dramatise this, but neither does he minimise it. Disciples today live in a culture that often equates blessing with comfort and success. Paul corrects this quietly but firmly. Suffering is not evidence that Christ has failed. It is often evidence that allegiance to Christ is real. To live faithfully is to remember suffering believers, pray for them, learn from them, and allow their endurance to strengthen our own resolve.

Fifth, Paul's chains call us to live with **courage grounded in Christ's sovereignty**. Paul is imprisoned, but the gospel is not. The very existence of this letter proves that Christ's purposes continue even when his servants are constrained. Disciples today can become discouraged when circumstances limit what they hoped to do for God. Paul reminds us that God's work is not fragile. When one avenue closes, another opens. Faithfulness is not defined by freedom of movement, but by trust and obedience where we are. To live faithfully is to serve Christ confidently even when our role feels reduced or unseen.

Sixth, Paul calls us to live with **grace as the sustaining atmosphere of discipleship**. His final word is not instruction, warning, or exhortation, but blessing: "Grace be with you." (Colossians 4:18). Grace is not merely how the Christian life begins. It is how it continues. Disciples today often attempt to persevere through sheer resolve, only to find themselves weary or discouraged. Paul reminds us that endurance is sustained by grace received daily. Grace frees us from despair when we fail, from pride when we succeed, and from fear when obedience is costly.

Seventh, this passage calls us to live with **a long-term vision of faithfulness rather than short-term results**. Everything in these final verses points toward endurance – Scripture read again and again, ministry completed over time, suffering borne patiently, grace relied upon continually. Paul is shaping a Church prepared not just for moments of crisis, but for decades of obedience. Discipleship today often falters because expectations are too short. We expect quick change, visible fruit, and immediate affirmation. Paul calls us instead to steady, resilient faith.

Finally, Colossians ends by reminding us that discipleship is lived **under the lordship of Christ until the end**. The letter that began with the supremacy of Christ ends with dependence on his grace. This is not accidental. Christ reigns. Christ sustains. Christ completes what he begins. To live faithfully today is to trust that truth when obedience feels ordinary, when service feels unnoticed, and when perseverance feels costly.

So how then shall we live? We live shaped by Scripture together. We complete what Christ has entrusted to us. We accept accountability and encouragement from the Church. We remember suffering believers and learn courage from them. We trust Christ's work even in limitation. We rely daily on grace. And we commit ourselves to long obedience under the lordship of Christ.

This is the quiet strength of mature discipleship. And it is enough – because grace truly is with us.

9. PERSEVERING IN THE WORK OF THE LORD
(Colossians 4:15-18)

As Paul reaches the closing lines of his letter, there is no sense of fading energy or diminished concern. Instead, these final verses gather together themes that have shaped the entire letter and place them firmly within the life of the Church. Perseverance, responsibility, shared ministry, and sustaining grace all come into sharp focus. What Paul has taught doctrinally and pastorally now settles into the lived rhythms of Christian community.

The gospel which Paul proclaims does not terminate in ideas. It produces a people who read God's word together, encourage one another to faithfulness, bear responsibility for ministry, and persevere under pressure. Colossians 4:15–18 shows us what enduring faith looks like when Christ is truly at the centre.

The Church beyond one local gathering

Paul begins by widening the horizon of the Colossians' vision. "Give my greetings to the brothers and sisters at Laodicea, and to Nympha and the Church in her house." (Colossians 4:15). The Church is immediately presented as being larger than one congregation or one location. Believers belong to a network of fellowship that transcends geography.

This reminder matters. The Colossians are not an isolated community carrying the weight of faithfulness alone. They are part of a wider body of Christ. Mutual recognition strengthens perseverance. Knowing that others are walking the same path fosters encouragement and accountability.

The reference to a Church meeting in a house draws attention to the ordinary settings in which early Christian life flourished. There were no dedicated Church buildings, no public recognition, and often no social approval. Yet the gospel took root in homes, among families and friends, shaped by hospitality and commitment. Nympha's mention highlights the importance of individuals who open their lives and resources for the sake of the gospel.

Hosting a Church was not a minor act of kindness. It involved risk, responsibility, and ongoing sacrifice. Paul honours such faithfulness. This reminds the Church that significant ministry very often happens quietly and locally. Faithfulness is expressed not only through preaching or travel, but through providing space where God's people can gather and grow.

The centrality of God's Word in the life of the Church

Paul now gives an instruction that reveals how deeply he values Scripture within the gathered community. "After this letter has been read to you, see that it is also read in the Church of the Laodiceans and that you in turn read the letter from Laodicea." (Colossians 4:16).

The public reading of Scripture is assumed, not debated. Paul expects his letter to be read aloud to the congregation. God's word is not reserved for a select few. It belongs to the whole Church. Hearing Scripture together shapes belief, strengthens unity, and forms shared understanding. Paul's instruction also highlights the shared responsibility of Churches toward one another. What one Church receives is meant to benefit others. The word of God is not to be hoarded or treated as private property. It is to circulate, instruct, and build up the wider body.

This exchange of letters underscores the communal nature of Christian growth. Believers mature not only through individual study, but through shared exposure to God's truth. The reading of Scripture together fosters accountability and shared obedience. Paul's concern here reflects his broader theology. Christ is supreme, and his word must therefore occupy a central place among his people. A Church that neglects Scripture weakens its ability to persevere. A Church that listens attentively to God's word is strengthened for faithful living.

A direct call to faithful ministry

Paul now turns to a specific individual within the community. "Tell Archippus: 'See to it that you complete the ministry you have received in the Lord.'" (Colossians 4:17).

This personal exhortation stands out sharply among the general greetings. Archippus is not singled out for criticism, but for encouragement and responsibility. Ministry is described as something received in the Lord. It is not self-appointed or self-generated. It is entrusted by Christ himself.

At the same time, that trust carries responsibility. To receive ministry is to be accountable for it. Paul urges completion, not perfection. The concern is faithfulness to the calling given, not comparison with others or pursuit of recognition. The public nature of this exhortation is significant. The Church is invited to support Archippus in his calling. Ministry is never exercised in isolation. Encouragement, accountability, and prayer from the community are essential to perseverance.

This moment also reminds the Church that leadership and service can at time be quite difficult. Weariness, opposition, and discouragement are real threats. Paul's words function as a strengthening reminder that the Lord who assigns ministry also sustains those who carry it.

Perseverance in the face of pressure

Paul's final personal words bring the letter to a poignant close. "I, Paul, write this greeting in my own hand. Remember my chains." (Colossians 4:18). By writing in his own hand, Paul underscores the authenticity and personal cost behind the letter. The reference to chains is brief but powerful. Paul does not elaborate or seek sympathy. He simply reminds the Church that faithfulness to Christ can involve suffering. The gospel does not promise ease. It promises purpose.

Paul's chains are not a contradiction of Christ's supremacy. They are an expression of allegiance to it. His imprisonment frames the entire letter as testimony that Christ reigns even when his servants suffer. This reminder also serves to steady the Church. If their apostle endures hardship without abandoning hope, they too can persevere in their calling. Faithfulness is sustained not by favourable circumstances, but by confidence in Christ's lordship.

Grace as the final word

Paul closes with a blessing that gathers the entire letter into a single word. "Grace be with you." (Colossians 4:18). Grace has shaped every chapter of the letter. Grace rescues. Grace reconciles. Grace transforms. Grace sustains. Paul does not end with instruction or warning, but with grace, because grace is what enables everything he has called the Church to do. Without grace, perseverance collapses into duty. With grace, obedience becomes response.

This final word reminds the Church that endurance is not achieved through strength alone. It is sustained through ongoing dependence on God's kindness and power. As this final sermon unfolds, the picture becomes clear. A persevering Church is one that stays rooted in God's word, supports faithful ministry, bears responsibility together, and lives under the sustaining grace of Christ.

Paul's letter ends as it began, with Christ at the centre. Where Christ reigns, grace flows. And where grace flows, God's people are enabled to persevere faithfully to the end.

As Paul's final instructions continue to settle in, the focus sharpens on the shared responsibility of the Church to preserve faithfulness over time.

These closing verses are not merely affectionate farewells. They are practical safeguards for perseverance. Paul understands that endurance in the Christian life does not happen accidentally. It is cultivated through shared practices, mutual accountability, and continual reliance on grace.

What is striking in this section is how deliberately Paul links perseverance to ordinary disciplines. Reading Scripture together, supporting those in ministry, remembering suffering believers, and living consciously under grace are not peripheral habits. They are essential means by which God sustains his people.

Scripture read, shared, and obeyed together

Paul's instruction concerning the circulation and public reading of letters reveals a great deal about how spiritual stability is formed. When Paul says that his letter is to be read publicly and exchanged with the Church in Laodicea (Colossians 4:16), he is reinforcing the communal nature of Christian growth. Faith is not sustained by private insight alone. The word of God must be heard together, interpreted together, and obeyed together. Public reading of Scripture ensures that the Word shapes the whole community rather than being filtered through personal preference or selective emphasis.

This practice also establishes a shared authority. When the Church gathers around the Word of God, no single voice dominates. The authority rests with God's revealed truth rather than with individual personalities. This guards the Church against drift and division.

Paul's insistence on sharing letters between Churches also highlights accountability beyond local boundaries. Churches are not free to reinvent the faith according to local taste. They are part of a wider body that listens to the same gospel and submits to the same Lord. This mutual exchange of Scripture strengthens perseverance by anchoring belief in something stable and external. When circumstances change or pressures intensify, the word of God remains a fixed reference point.

Ministry as a trust to be completed

Paul's exhortation to Archippus takes on greater weight when read in this context. "See to it that you complete the ministry you have received in the Lord." (Colossians 4:17). Ministry is presented not as a personal project, but as a trust entrusted by Christ. Completion here does not imply perfection or dramatic success. It implies faithfulness. Ministry may unfold quietly, slowly, and with limited visible fruit. Paul's concern is not with outcomes, but with obedience to the calling given. This exhortation reminds the Church that ministry is not sustained by enthusiasm alone. There are seasons of weariness when the temptation to disengage becomes strong.

Paul's words function as a steadying reminder that the Lord who assigns ministry also watches over it. The public nature of this charge also matters. Archippus is not left to shoulder this responsibility alone. The Church is called to support him, encourage him, and hold him accountable. Perseverance in ministry is a communal effort. This dynamic applies broadly. Every believer entrusted with responsibility, whether visible or hidden, requires encouragement to continue. The Church must cultivate a culture that values long-term faithfulness rather than short-term excitement.

Remembering chains and bearing one another's burdens

Paul's brief request, "Remember my chains." (Colossians 4:18), brings suffering into the centre of the Church's consciousness. Paul does not elaborate or dramatise his imprisonment. He simply asks to be remembered. This remembrance is not sentimental. It is practical and spiritual. To remember Paul's chains is to pray for him, to draw courage from his example, and to remain committed to the gospel he suffers for.

Paul's chains also function as a sobering reminder of the cost of discipleship. Faithfulness to Christ can lead to hardship, misunderstanding, and loss. The Church must not be naïve about this reality. Perseverance requires realism.

the same time, Paul's chains are not presented as evidence of failure. They are evidence of faithfulness. Christ's supremacy is not diminished by the suffering of his servants. It is often displayed through it. By calling the Church to remember his chains, Paul invites them into shared burden-bearing. Suffering is not to be borne alone. The Church stands together, supporting one another through prayer, encouragement, and solidarity.

Grace as the environment of perseverance

Paul's final blessing continues to echo throughout this section. "Grace be with you." (Colossians 4:18). Grace is not merely the starting point of the Christian life. It is the environment in which perseverance becomes possible.

Without grace, the call to faithfulness can become crushing. Responsibilities feel heavy. Suffering feels unbearable. Scripture feels demanding. Within an environment of grace, obedience can become response, endurance can become hope-filled, and suffering will become meaningful.

God's grace reminds the Church that perseverance is not self-generated. It is sustained by God's ongoing provision. The same grace that reconciled believers to God continues to strengthen them for faithful living. This emphasis protects the Church from legalism and despair. Perseverance is not achieved through relentless effort alone. It is nurtured through continual dependence on God's kindness and power. Paul's final word therefore gathers the entire letter into a single sustaining truth. Christ is supreme. His grace is sufficient. Everything the Church is called to do flows from that reality.

Perseverance as a shared calling

When these elements are held together, a clear pattern emerges. Perseverance is cultivated through shared Scripture, supported ministry, remembered suffering, and sustained grace. None of these stand alone. Together, they form a resilient framework for faithful Christian life.

The Church that listens attentively to God's word is anchored in truth. The Church that supports those in ministry resists discouragement. The Church that remembers suffering believers grows in courage. The Church that lives by grace remains hopeful. Paul's closing instructions are therefore deeply pastoral. He does not simply urge endurance. He shows how God provides the means for it. Perseverance is not left to human strength. It is shaped by God's provision through ordinary practices.

As the letter draws nearer to its final word, the Colossians are invited to see themselves as participants in a larger story of faithfulness. They are not merely recipients of teaching. They are bearers of responsibility, called to live out what they have received.

In the midst of pressure, uncertainty, and opposition, the Apostle Paul's message remains steady. Continue. Complete the ministry entrusted to you. Listen to God's word together. Remember those who suffer. And rely always on the grace that Christ supplies. This is how the Church endures. This is how faithfulness is sustained. And this is how the supremacy of Christ is honoured in the long obedience of everyday life.

As Paul brings this letter to its close, the final verses gather the life of the Church into a single, sustained call: persevere together under the grace and lordship of Christ. There is no new teaching introduced here. Instead, Paul presses the implications of everything he has already said. The supremacy of Christ, the sufficiency of his work, the new life believers share in him, and the wisdom required for faithful living now converge in these last exhortations. What emerges is a vision of Christian endurance that is communal, realistic, and deeply hopeful.

Perseverance rooted in shared responsibility

Paul's instructions assume that perseverance is not an individual achievement. It is a shared responsibility. Churches greet one another, share Scripture with one another, and support one another in ministry. This mutuality guards believers against isolation, which so often leads to discouragement.

By urging the Colossians to exchange letters with the Church in Laodicea (Colossians 4:16), Paul reinforces the idea that no Church exists for itself alone. Exposure to the same apostolic teaching binds congregations together in a common faith and a common direction. Perseverance is strengthened when believers know they are not alone in their struggles or convictions.

This shared responsibility also keeps the Church anchored. When Scripture is read publicly and received collectively, it shapes not only personal devotion but communal identity. The Church learns together what it means to live under Christ's lordship. In those times of pressure or confusion, this shared grounding becomes a stabilising force.

Paul understands that drifting often happens quietly. A Church that stops listening together to God's word gradually loses clarity and confidence. By contrast, a Church that gathers around Scripture together is continually reoriented toward truth.

Completing the work entrusted by the Lord

Paul's exhortation to Archippus continues to resonate as the letter closes. "See to it that you complete the ministry you have received in the Lord." (Colossians 4:17). This is not simply a personal charge. It is representative of the responsibility every believer carries. Ministry, in whatever form it takes, is something received, not invented. It comes from the Lord. That reality both dignifies and sobers. What Christ entrusts matters. It deserves perseverance.

Completion does not mean flawless execution or visible success. It means faithful continuation. Paul does not urge Archippus to innovate or expand. He urges him to finish what he has been given. In a culture that often celebrates beginnings more than endurance, this word is deeply countercultural. The Church's role in this is implied. Public exhortation invites public support. Archippus is not left alone to muster resolve. The community is called to stand with him, encouraging him to continue when the work becomes heavy or unseen.

This dynamic reflects a broader truth. Perseverance in Christian service is sustained through encouragement and accountability. Believers are strengthened when others recognise their calling and remind them of the Lord who gave it.

Suffering remembered without shame

Paul's brief appeal, "Remember my chains." (Colossians 4:18), places suffering squarely within the life of the Church. Paul does not explain his imprisonment or justify it. He simply asks to be remembered. This remembrance is significant. It keeps the cost of discipleship visible. The gospel Paul proclaims is worth suffering for. His chains are not an embarrassment. They are a testimony to faithfulness.

Remembering Paul's chains also guards the Church against a shallow understanding of perseverance. Endurance is not measured by ease or by comfort. Faithfulness often involves limitation, loss, or misunderstanding. Paul does not want the Colossians to forget this reality. At the same time, Paul's chains are not presented as a reason for despair. They are framed within confidence in Christ's lordship. Paul is imprisoned, but Christ is not. The gospel is not hindered. The letter itself is evidence of that. By remembering Paul's chains, the Church learns how to interpret suffering rightly. Suffering does not negate Christ's reign. It often displays it.

Grace as the sustaining power of the Christian life

Paul's final words bring everything into focus. "Grace be with you." (Colossians 4:18). This is not a polite closing. It is a theological conclusion. Grace is the environment in which perseverance happens. Grace is the empowering presence of God. Without grace, responsibility becomes crushing, Scripture becomes burdensome, and suffering becomes unbearable. With grace, obedience becomes response, endurance becomes hopeful, and suffering becomes meaningful. Throughout this whole letter, Paul has shown that believers are complete in Christ. That completeness does not remove the need for effort or faithfulness. It makes them possible. Grace does not replace perseverance. It sustains it.

Grace also levels the ground. Leaders and congregations, those who suffer and those who support, those who teach and those who listen all stand in the same need of grace. Perseverance is not achieved by spiritual elites. It is sustained by grace given to ordinary believers. Paul's closing blessing reminds the Church that everything he has called them to do depends on God's continued generosity. Grace is not a one-time gift at conversion. It is the daily provision by which believers continue.

A Church formed for long obedience

Taken together, these final verses present a vision of the Church shaped for long obedience rather than quick success. Scripture is read together.

Ministry is now completed faithfully. Suffering is remembered honestly. Grace is relied upon continually. This is how the Church endures. Not through constant innovation or dramatic moments, but through steady faithfulness rooted in Christ.

Paul does not end by urging the Colossians to achieve more. He urges them to remain. Remain in the word. Remain in the work given. Remain in solidarity with those who suffer. Remain under grace. The letter that began with the supremacy of Christ ends with the sufficiency of his grace. Christ reigns. His word instructs. His grace sustains. For the Colossians, and for the Church today, the call is clear. Live faithfully together under Christ's lordship. Bear responsibility with humility. Endure hardship with hope. And rely always on the grace that Christ supplies. This is not merely how a letter ends. It is how a Christian life continues.

How then shall we live?

Colossians 4:15–18 brings the letter to a close, but it does not wind discipleship down. Instead, Paul presses the life of faith into its most enduring shape: perseverance rooted in Scripture, responsibility embraced within community, suffering remembered honestly, and grace relied upon continually. For disciples of Christ today, this final passage calls us to a long obedience sustained not by intensity, but by faithfulness under Christ's lordship.

First, this passage calls us to live as people who are **shaped by God's word together, not in isolation**. Paul's instruction that his letter be read publicly and shared with neighbouring Churches (Colossians 4:16) reminds us that Scripture is fundamentally communal. Discipleship today often becomes individualised, reduced to private reading detached from shared accountability. Paul envisions something richer.

The word of Christ is meant to be heard, wrestled with, and obeyed together. To live faithfully now is to resist a pick-and-choose approach to Scripture and to commit ourselves to being formed by God's word within the gathered people of God.

This includes listening humbly, allowing Scripture to challenge cherished assumptions, and submitting our lives to its authority rather than merely using it for inspiration or affirmation.

Second, Paul calls us to live with **responsibility toward the ministries entrusted to us**. His direct word to Archippus – "See to it that you complete the ministry you have received in the Lord." (4:17) – is not only personal but representative. Every disciple has received some form of calling, responsibility, or trust from Christ. It may not be public or prominent, but it is real.

To live faithfully today is to take that calling very seriously. Completion matters. In a culture that celebrates beginnings and novelty, Paul reminds us that faithfulness is measured by perseverance. Discipleship is not proven by how enthusiastically we start, but by how faithfully we continue.

Third, this passage challenges us to always live with **mutual accountability as well as private spirituality**. Paul's exhortation to Archippus is delivered through the Church. This implies that perseverance in ministry is not meant to be solitary. Disciples today often struggle alone, quietly questioning whether their service still matters or whether they should continue. Paul shows us a better way. The Church is called to speak encouragement, offer reminder, and provide support so that believers do not abandon what Christ has entrusted to them. To live faithfully now is to allow others to speak into our calling and to accept encouragement as God's provision rather than personal intrusion.

Fourth, Paul calls us to live with **a sober and honest view of suffering**. His simple appeal, "Remember my chains." (Colossians 4:18), anchors discipleship in reality. Faithfulness to Christ may involve limitation, misunderstanding, or cost. Paul does not dramatise this, but neither does he minimise it. Disciples today live in a culture that often equates blessing with comfort and success. Paul corrects this quietly but firmly. Suffering is not evidence that Christ has failed. It is often evidence that allegiance to Christ is real.

To live faithfully is to remember suffering believers, pray for them, learn from them, and allow their endurance to strengthen our own resolve.

Fifth, Paul's chains call us to live with **courage grounded in Christ's sovereignty**. Paul is imprisoned, but the gospel is not. The very existence of this letter proves that Christ's purposes continue even when his servants are constrained. Disciples today can become discouraged when circumstances limit what they hoped to do for God. Paul reminds us that God's work is not fragile. When one avenue closes, another opens. Faithfulness is not defined by freedom of movement, but by trust and obedience where we are. To live faithfully is to serve Christ confidently even when our role feels reduced or unseen.

Sixth, Paul calls us to live with **grace as the sustaining atmosphere of discipleship**. His final word is not instruction, warning, or exhortation, but blessing: "Grace be with you." (Colossians 4:18). Grace is not merely how the Christian life begins. It is how it continues. Disciples today often attempt to persevere through sheer resolve, only to find themselves weary or discouraged. Paul reminds us that endurance is sustained by grace received daily. Grace frees us from despair when we fail, from pride when we succeed, and from fear when obedience is costly.

Seventh, this passage calls us to live with **a long-term vision of faithfulness rather than short-term results**. Everything in these final verses points toward endurance – Scripture read again and again, ministry completed over time, suffering borne patiently, grace relied upon continually. Paul is shaping a Church prepared not just for moments of crisis, but for decades of obedience. Discipleship today often falters because expectations are too short. We expect quick change, visible fruit, and immediate affirmation. Paul calls us instead to steady, resilient faith.

Finally, Colossians ends by reminding us that discipleship is lived **under the lordship of Christ until the end**. The letter that began with the supremacy of Christ ends with dependence on his grace.

This is not accidental. Christ reigns. Christ sustains. Christ completes what He begins. To live faithfully today is to trust that truth when obedience feels ordinary, when perseverance feels costly and when service feels unnoticed.

So how then shall we live?

⇒ We live shaped by Scripture together. We complete what Christ has entrusted to us.

⇒ We accept accountability and encouragement from the Church. We remember suffering believers and learn courage from them. We trust Christ's work even in limitation.

⇒ We rely daily on grace.

⇒ And we commit ourselves to long obedience under the lordship of Christ.

This is the quiet strength of mature discipleship. And it is enough – because grace truly is with us.

The message of Colossians continues wherever Christ is brought back to the centre of life. In every generation, there are new distractions, new voices, and new pressures that seek to redefine truth and reshape faith. Yet the answer remains the same as it was for the believers in Colossae. Christ is not one voice among many. He is not an addition to life, nor an enhancement to what we already are. He is the beginning, the foundation, and the fullness. To know Christ rightly is to see everything differently. Identity is no longer uncertain, because it is anchored in him. Growth is driven by abiding rather than striving. Community is no longer fragile, because it is held together in love and shaped by God's grace. Even the ordinary moments of life take on new meaning when lived under His lordship.

There is a quiet but profound freedom in all this. When Christ is truly above all, we are released from the burden of trying to hold everything together. We are no longer enslaved to comparison, defined by success, or shaken by circumstances. Our lives find stability, not in what we control, but in the One who reigns.

This also reshapes how we engage with the world around us. We no longer withdraw, and nor do we conform. Instead, we live with clarity and conviction, reflecting the character of Christ in the midst of everyday life. The gospel is not confined to words alone; it is seen in patience, in forgiveness, in humility, and in unwavering hope. This is the quiet power of Colossians. It does not call for something new, but for something true. Not a more complex faith, but a more centred one.

Where Christ is diminished, everything else becomes unstable. Where He is honoured, everything else finds its place. The call, then, is not complicated. It is clear and enduring. To live with Christ above all is to live with clarity, confidence, and purpose. It is to stand firm when the world shifts, and to remain anchored when other foundations give way. In the end, it is to discover that Christ is not only above all - but more than enough for all.

www.ingramcontent.com/pod-product-compliance
Lightning Source LLC
Chambersburg PA
CBHW072042150726
47996CB00014B/423